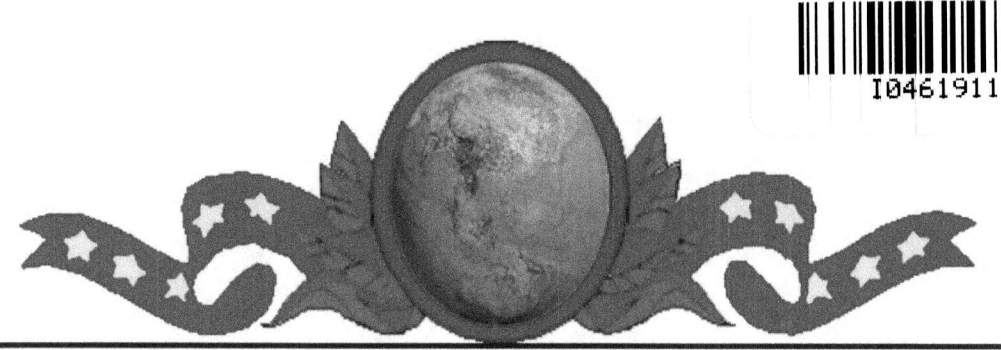

Real World
Colouring Book
For Advanced Users & Adults

Copyright 2019 By John Boom

50 Images

Created From Real Life Photos
For You To Colour As You Please.

ISBN 978-0-359-78840-8

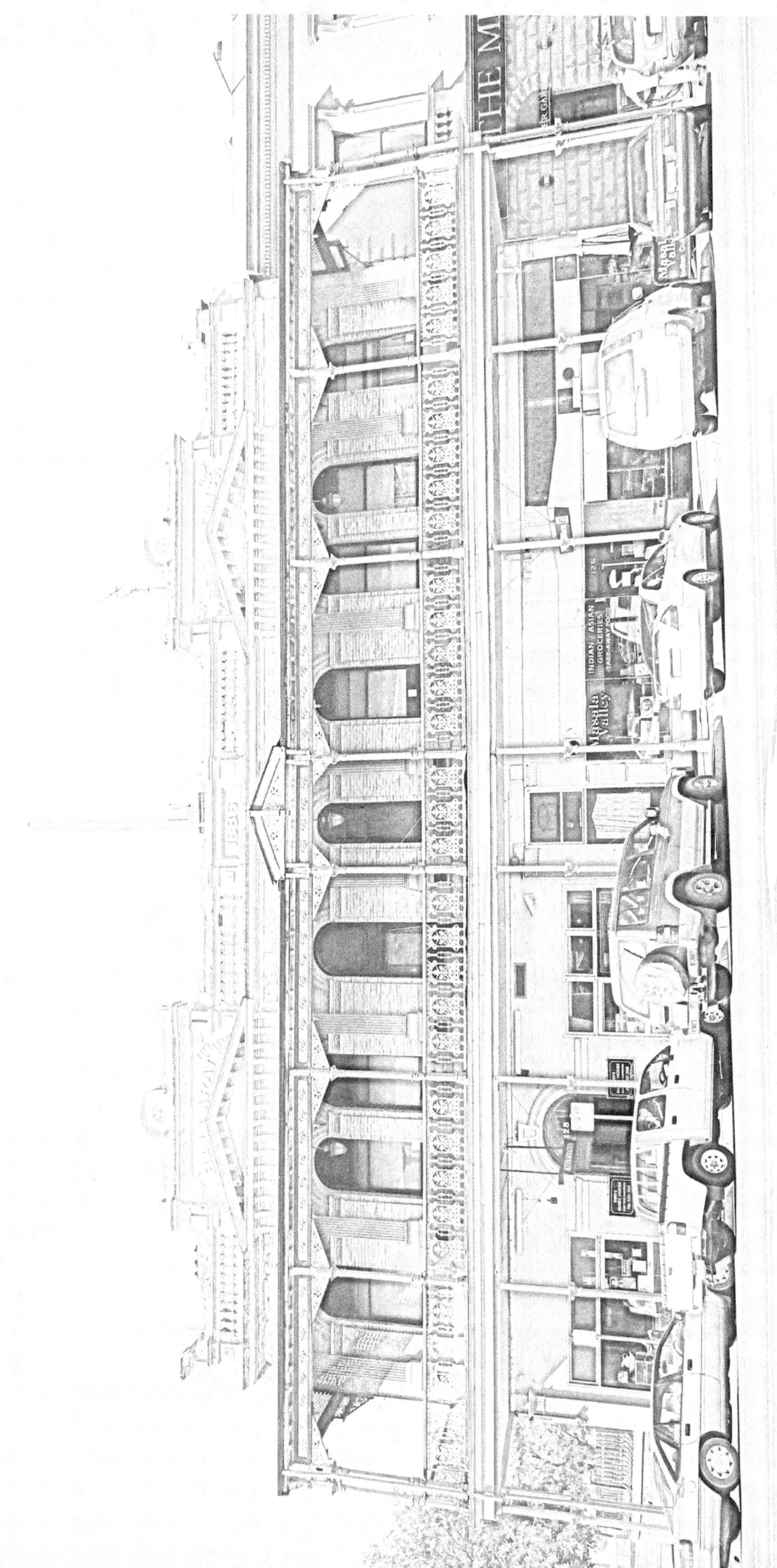

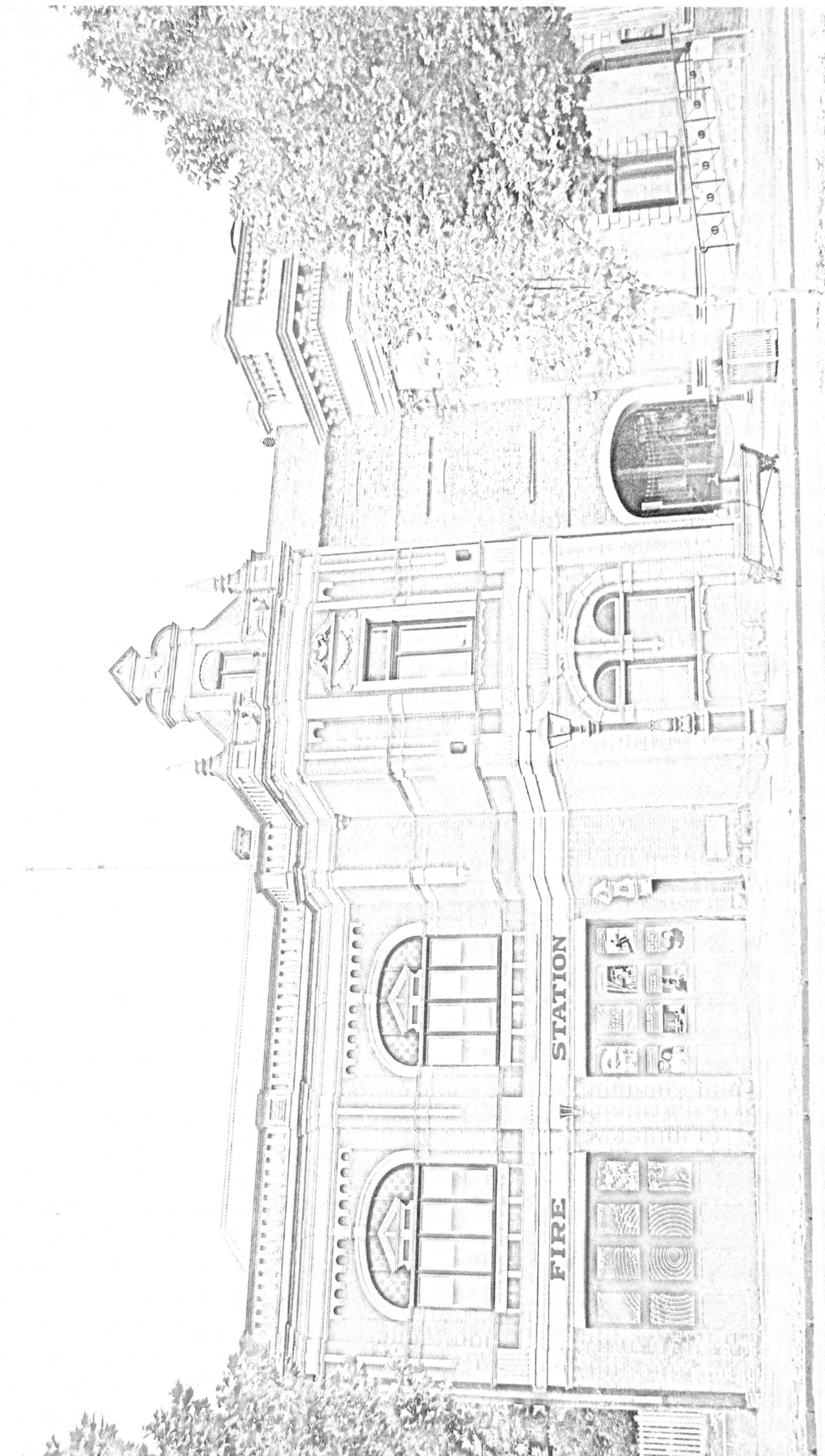

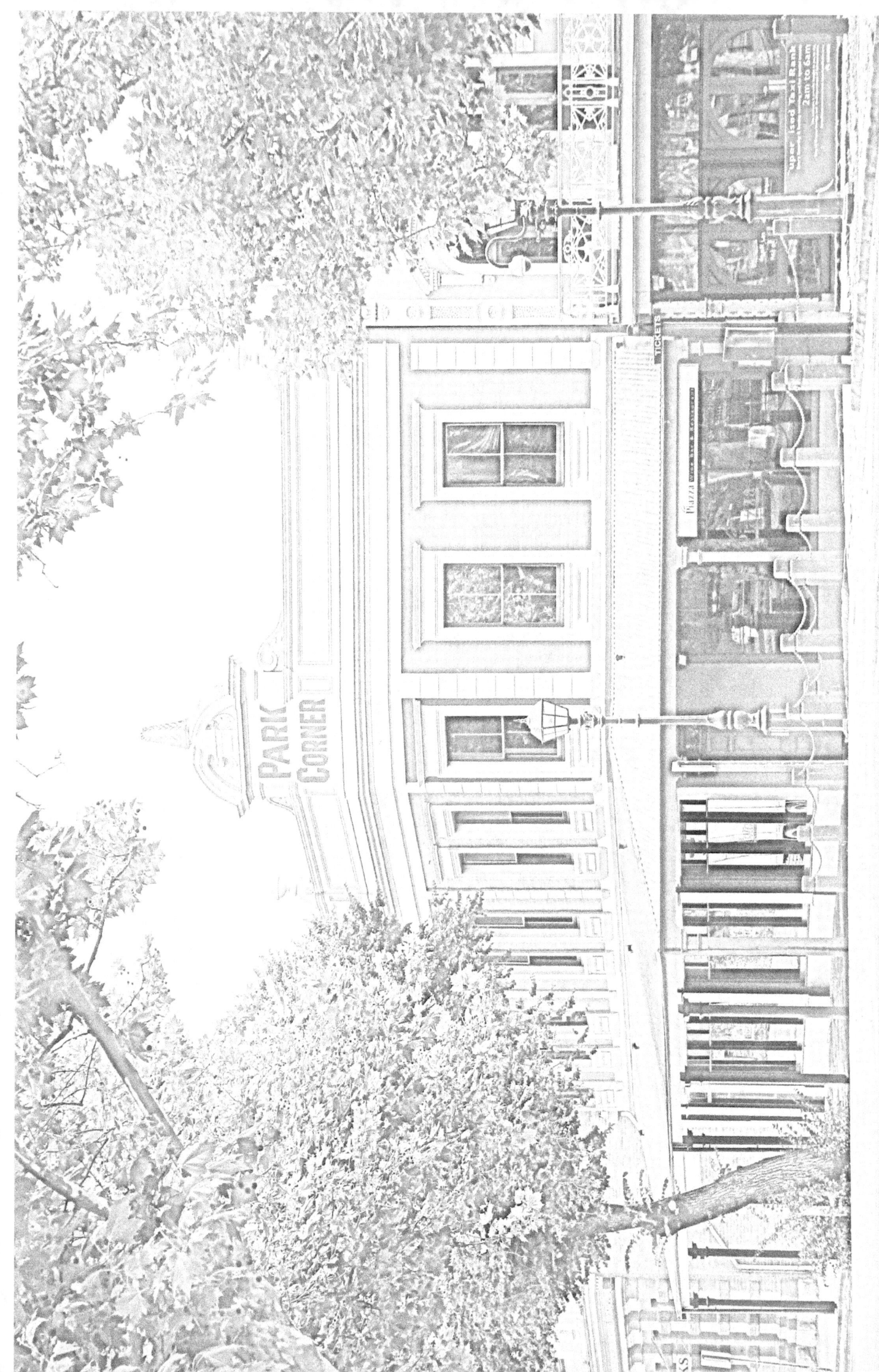

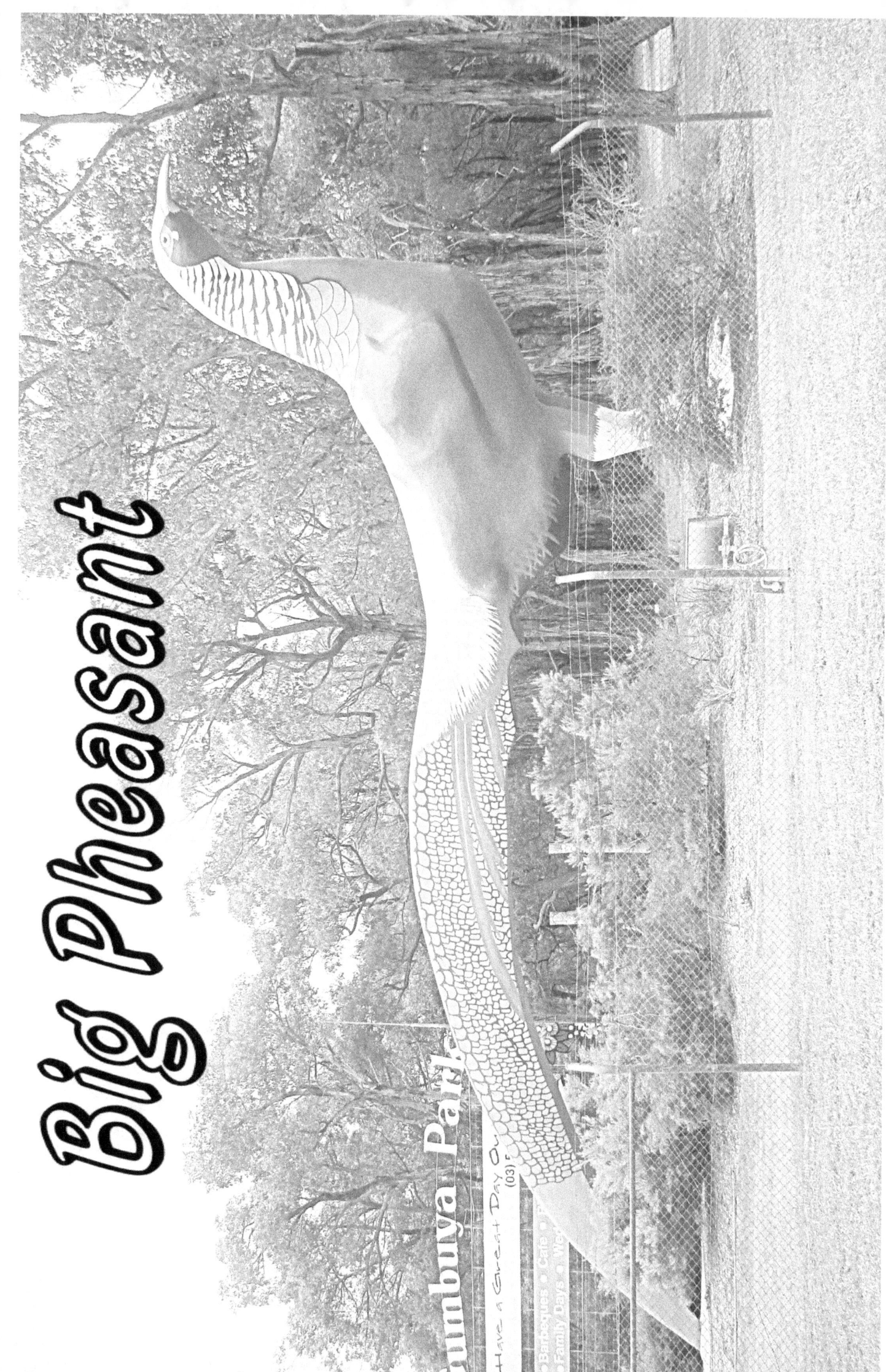

Big Pheeasant

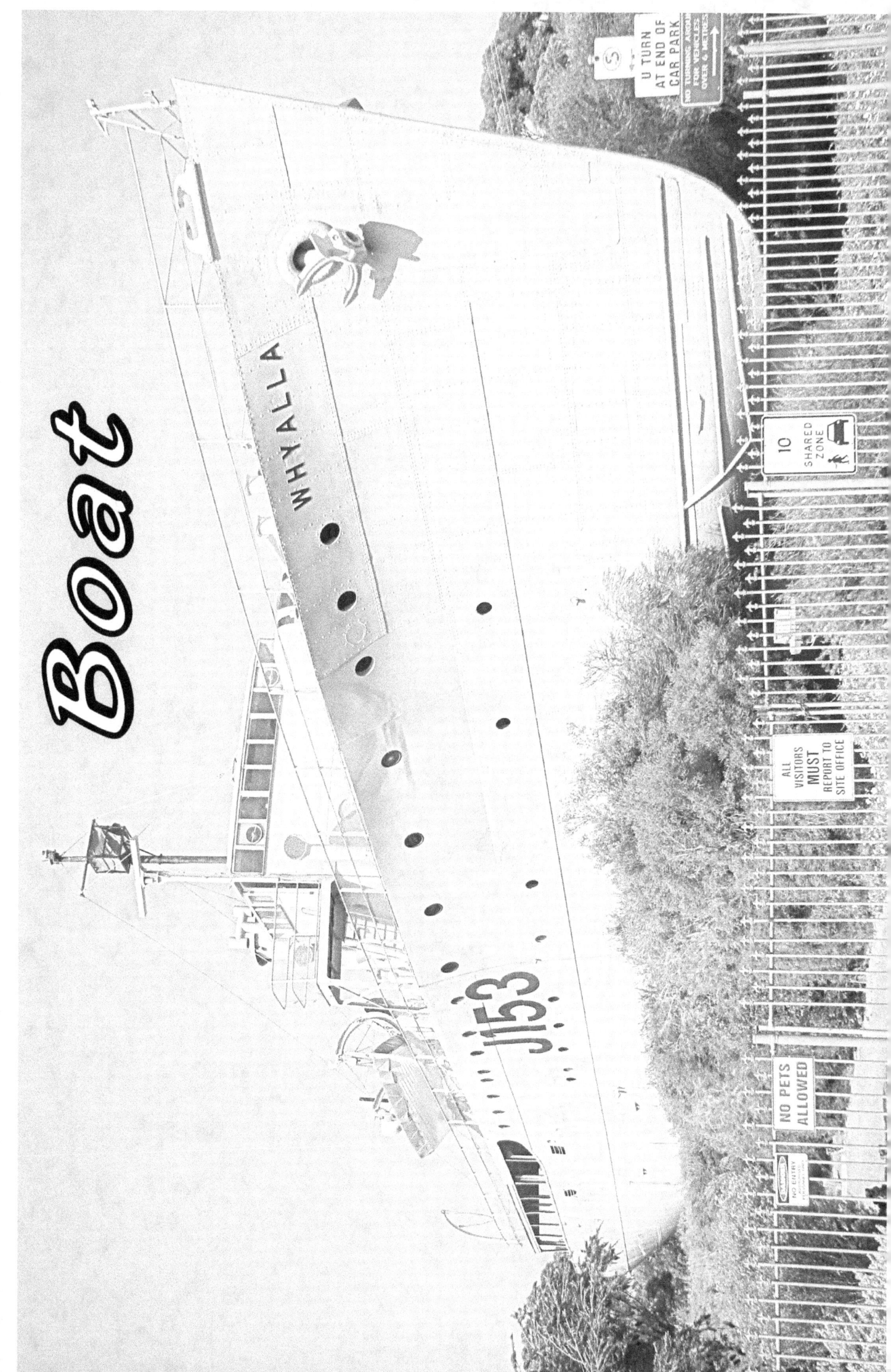

Boat

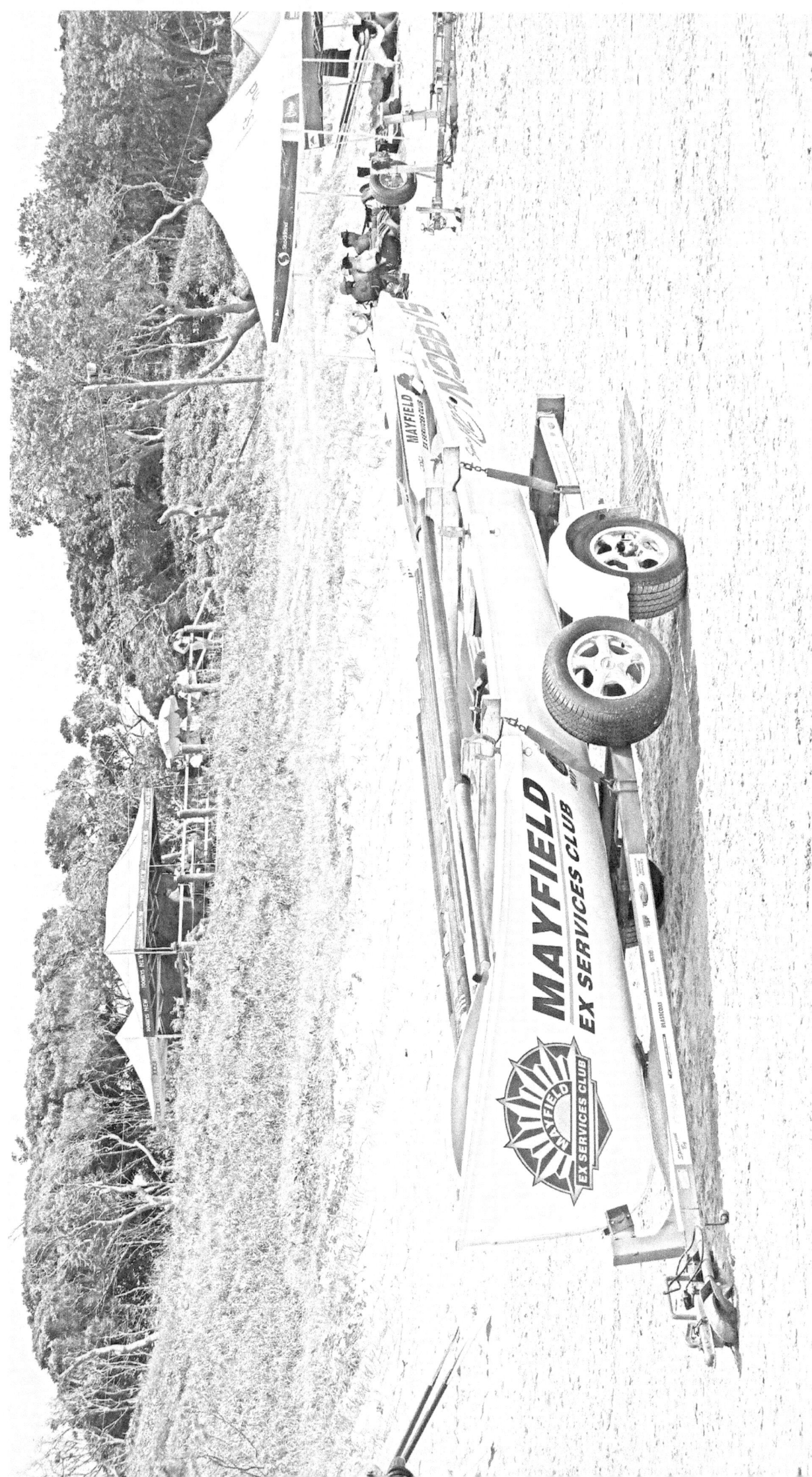

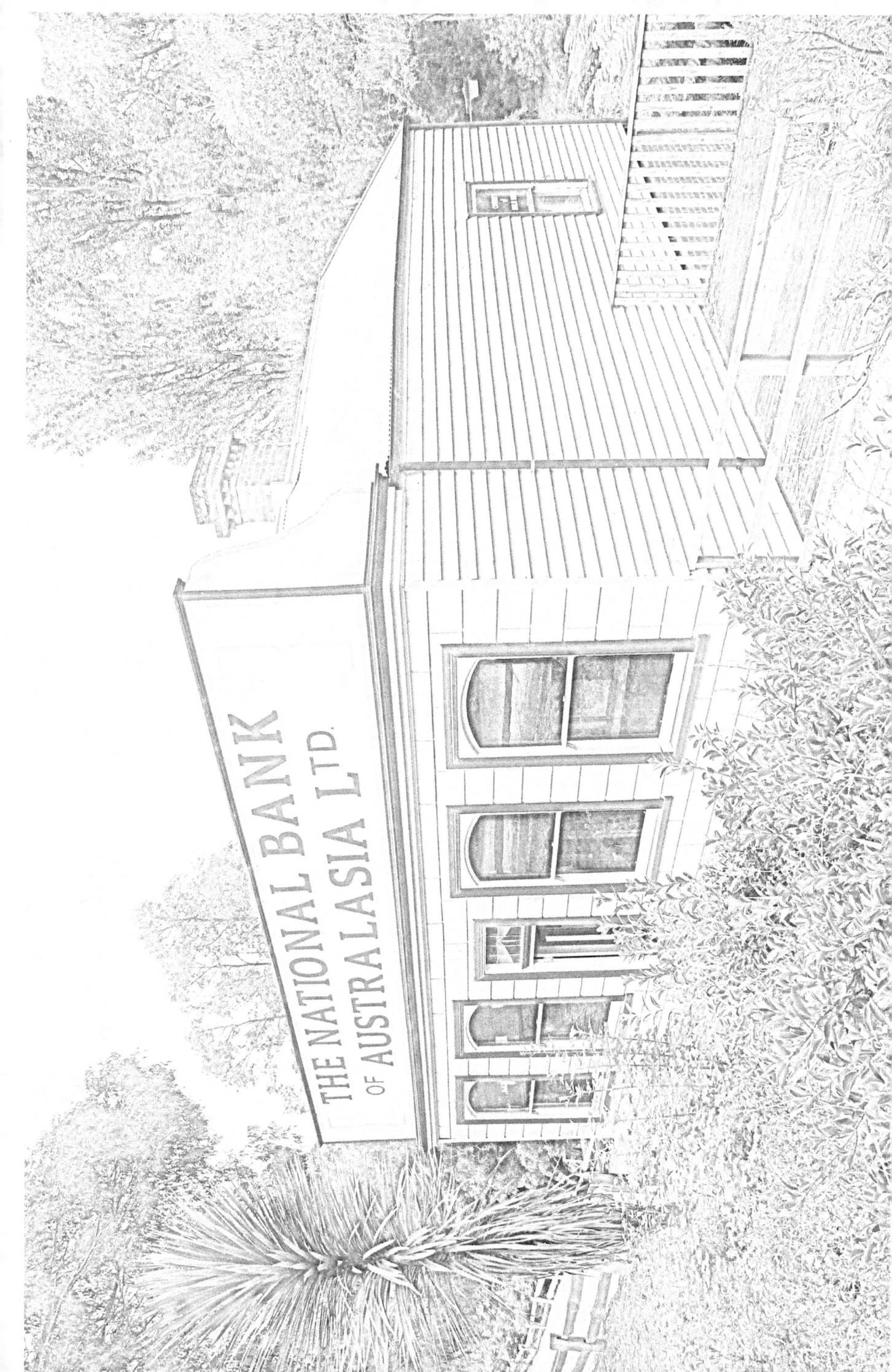

Harlequin Bugs

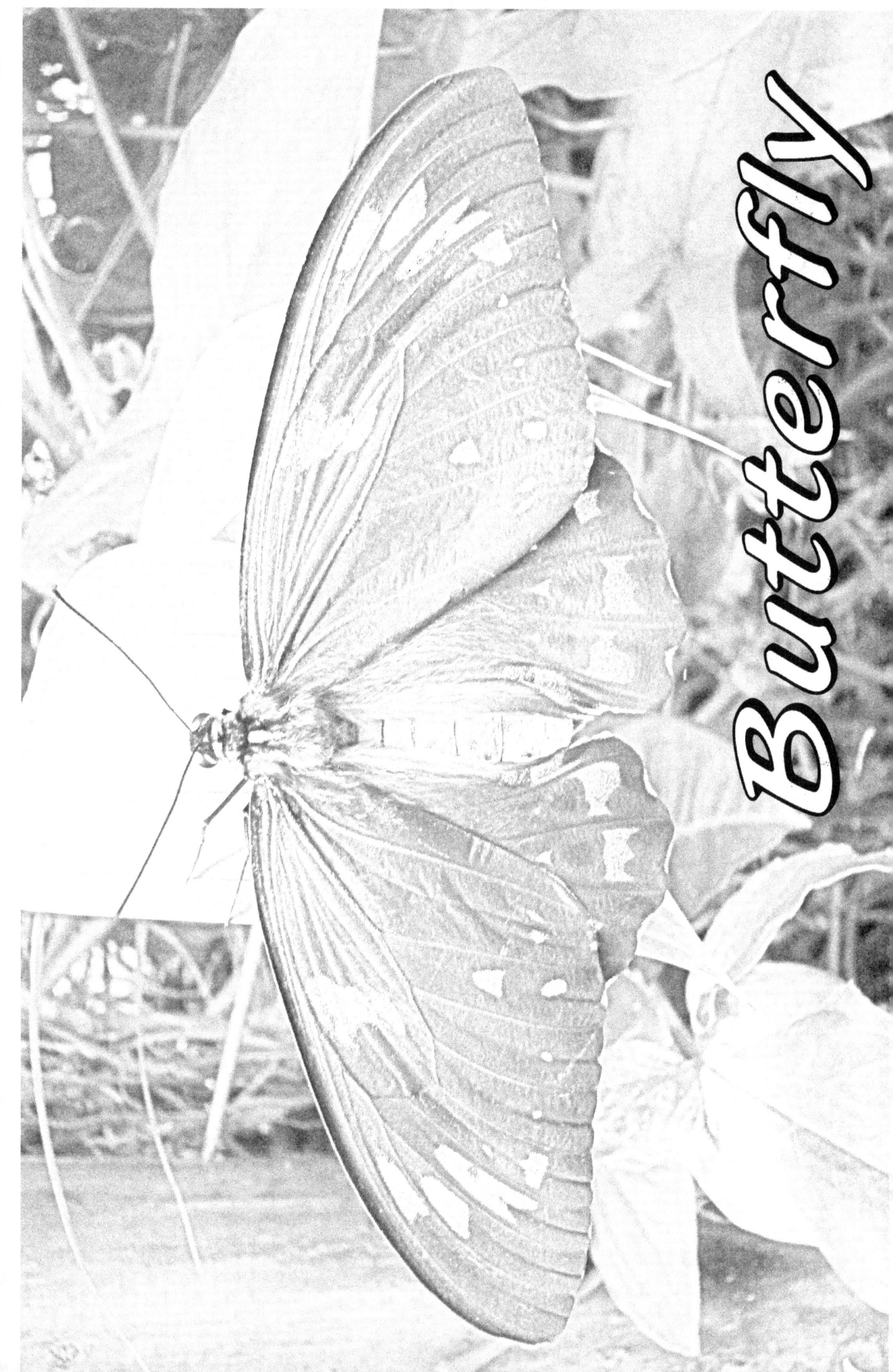

Butterfly

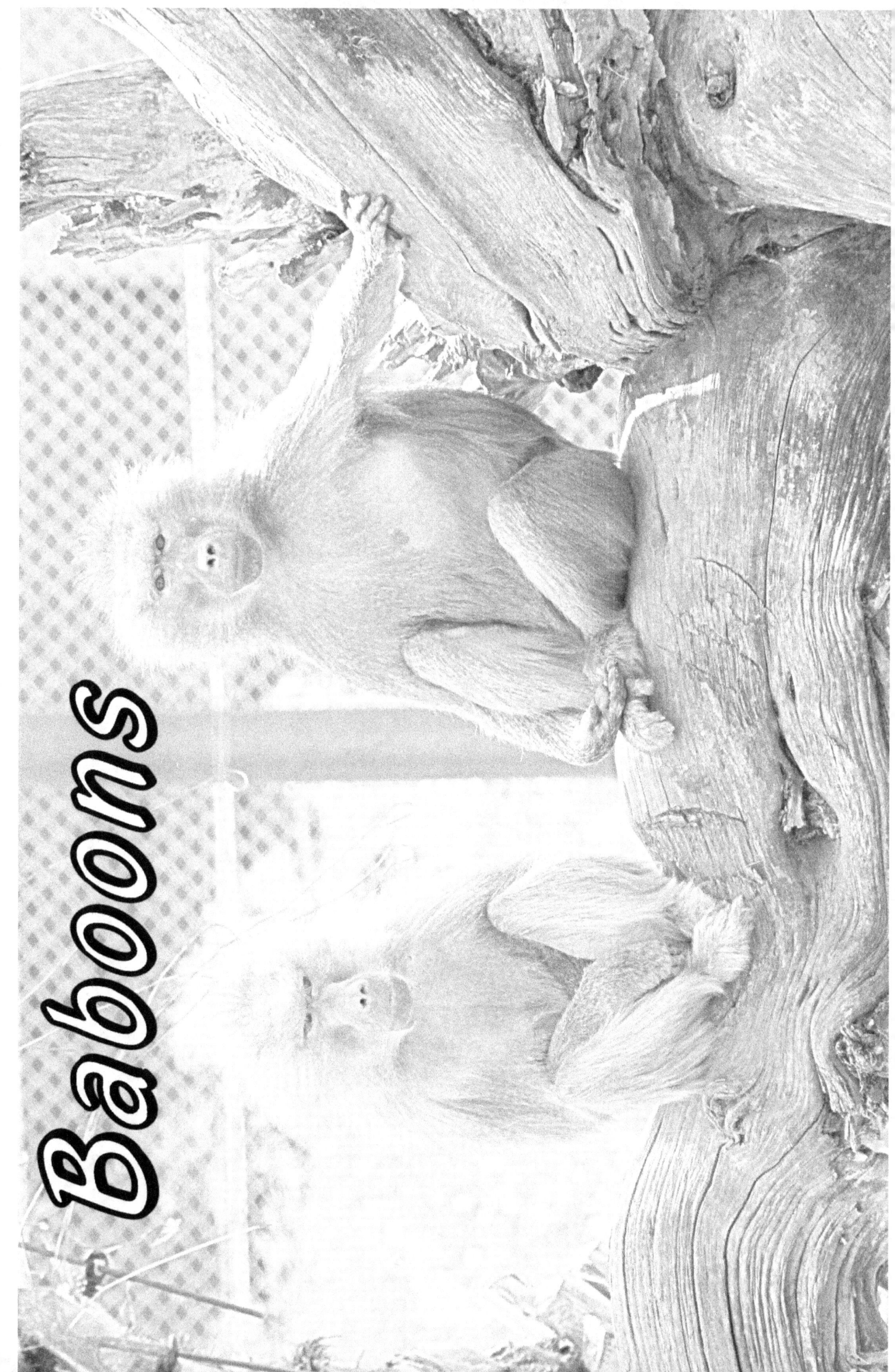

Baboons

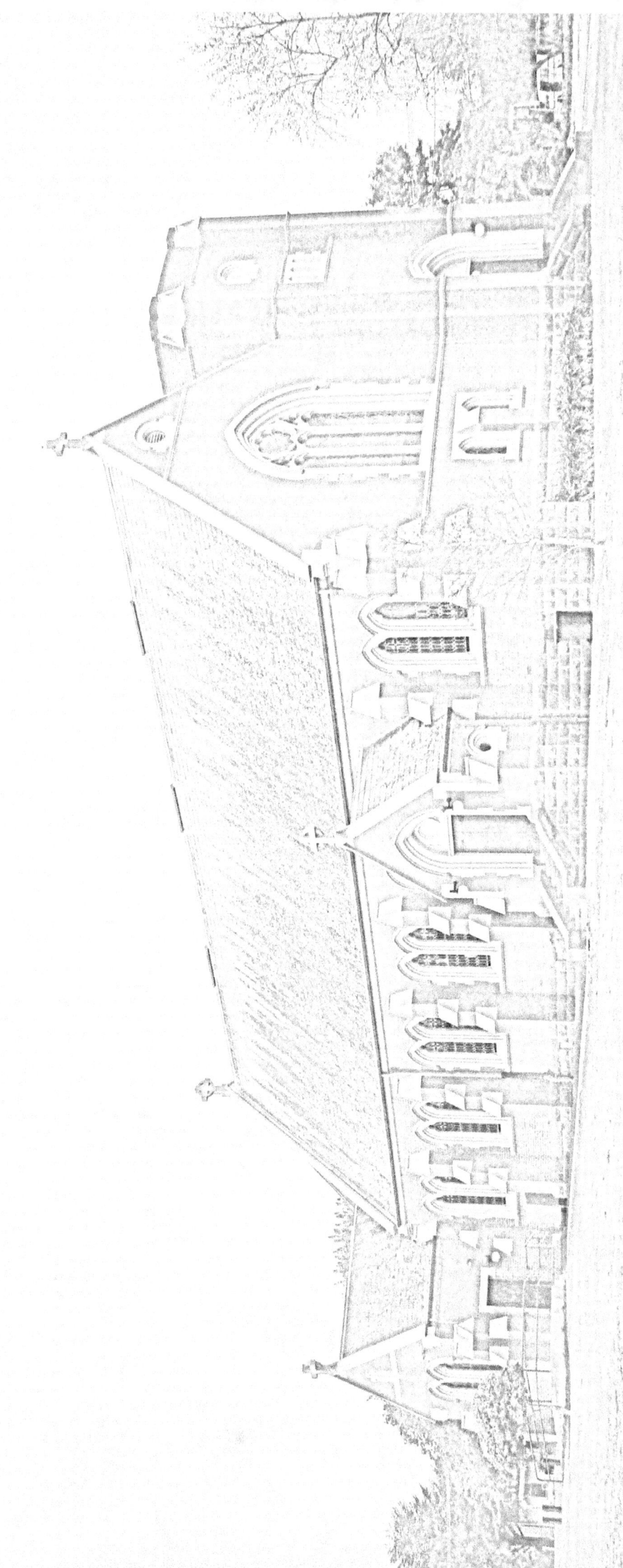

Church

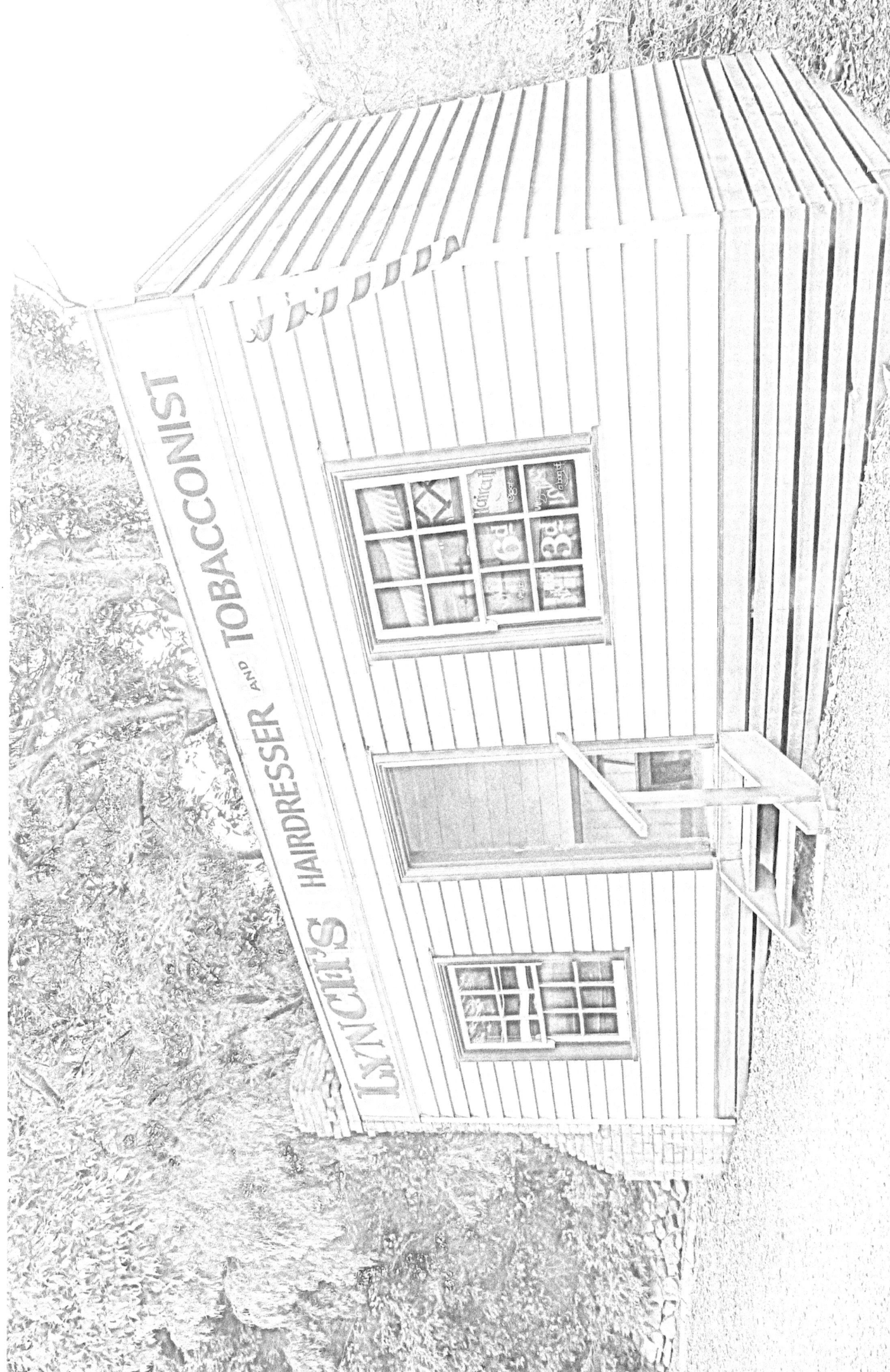

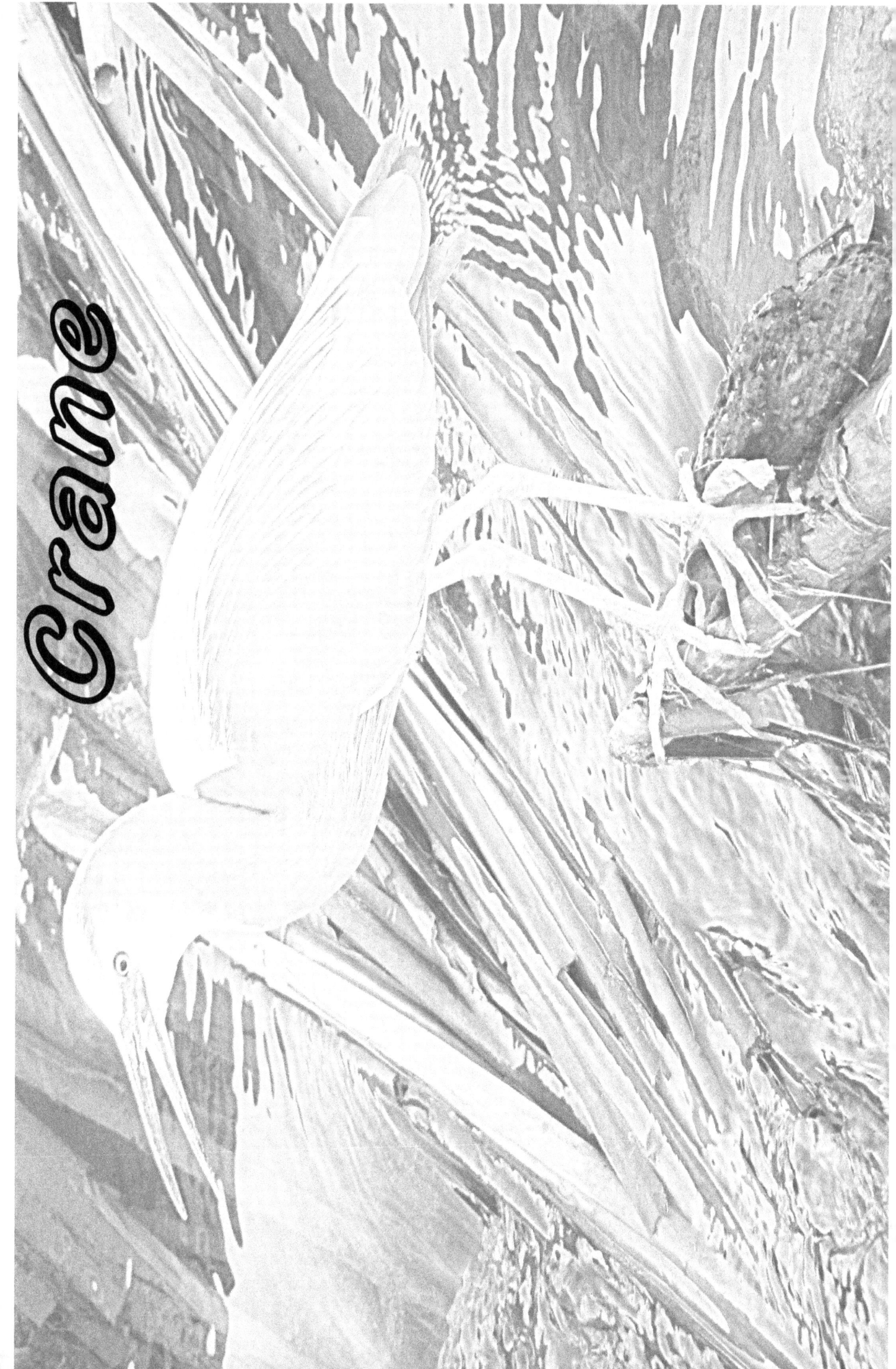

Crane

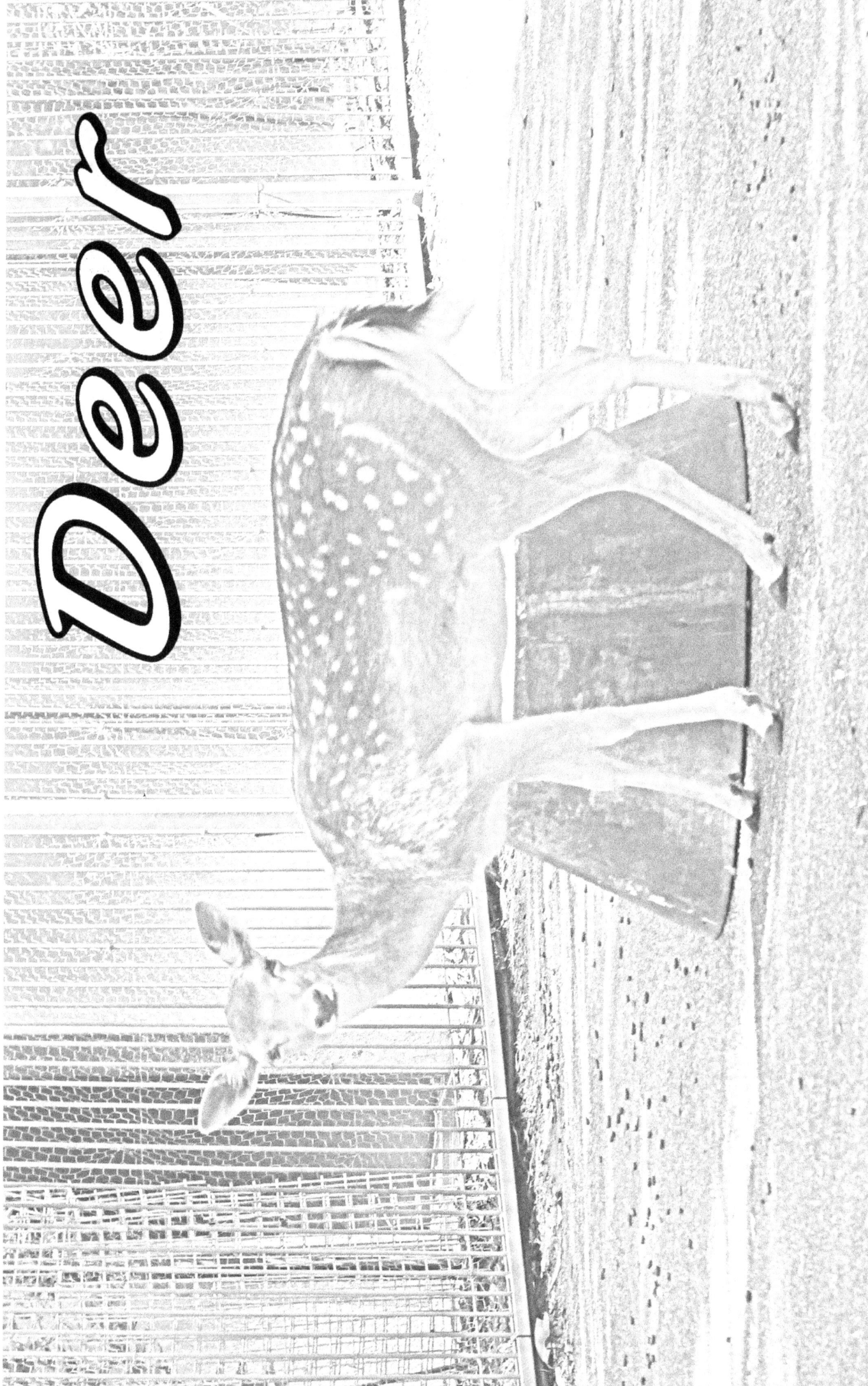

Deer

Echidna

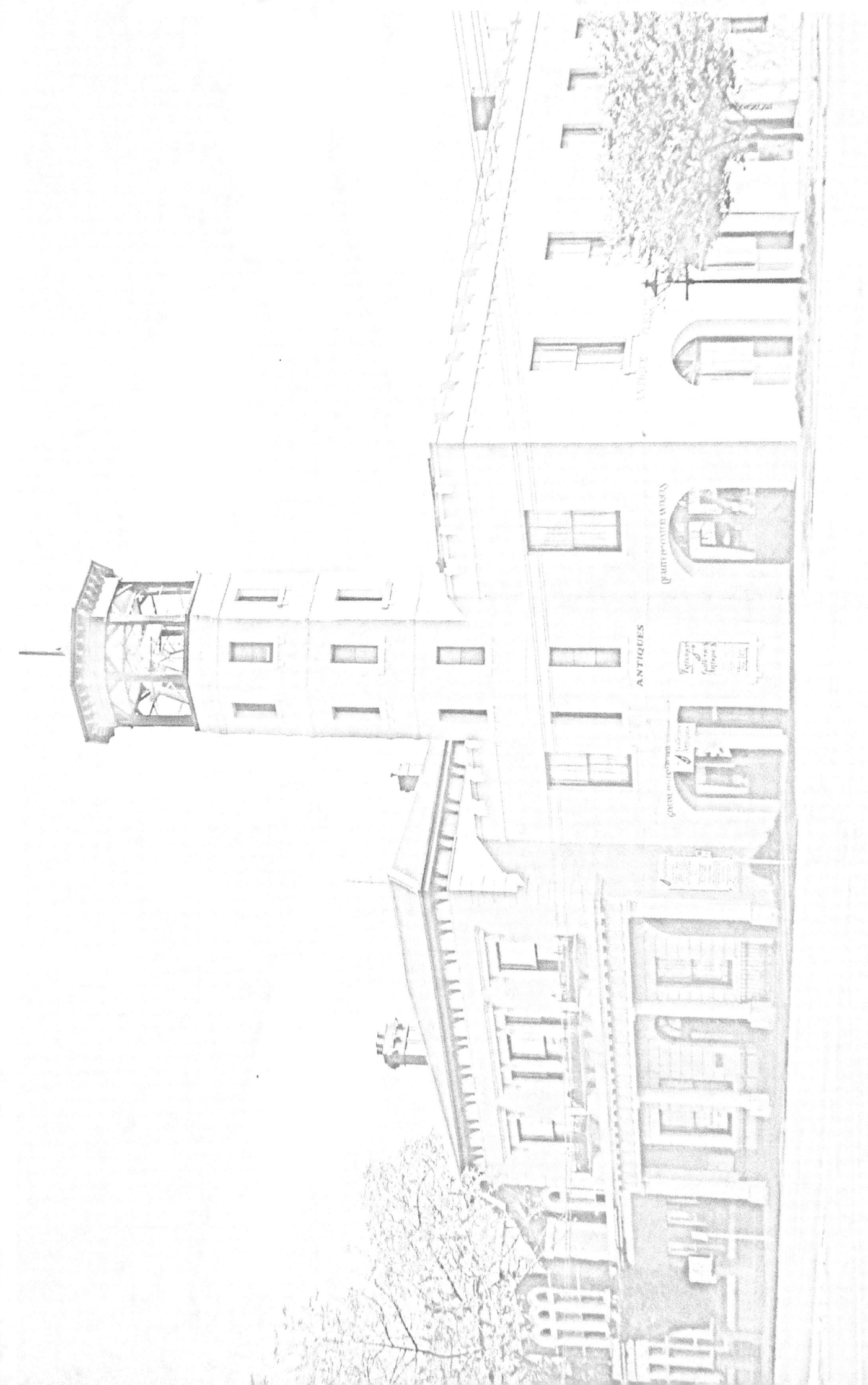

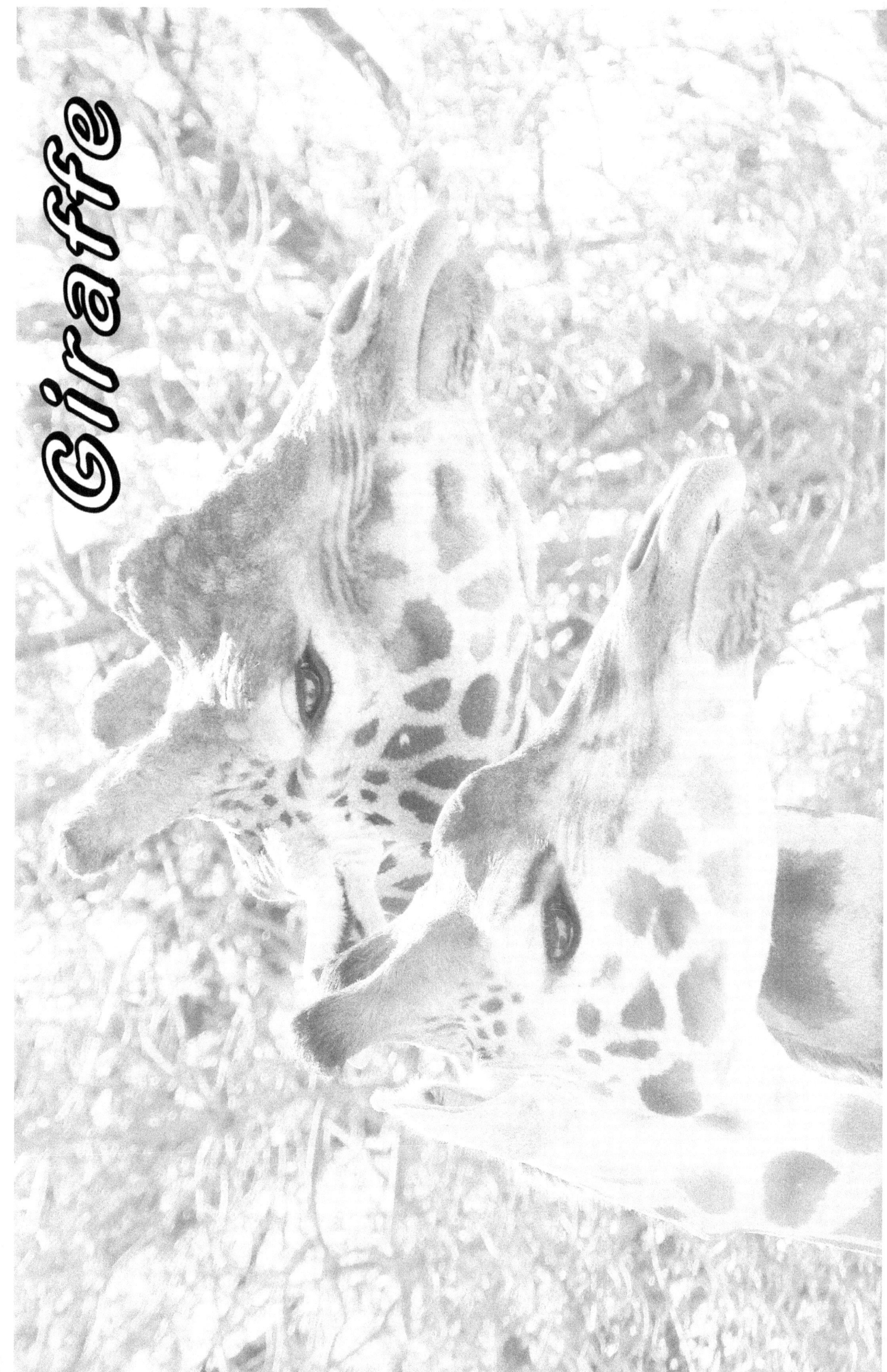

Hotel

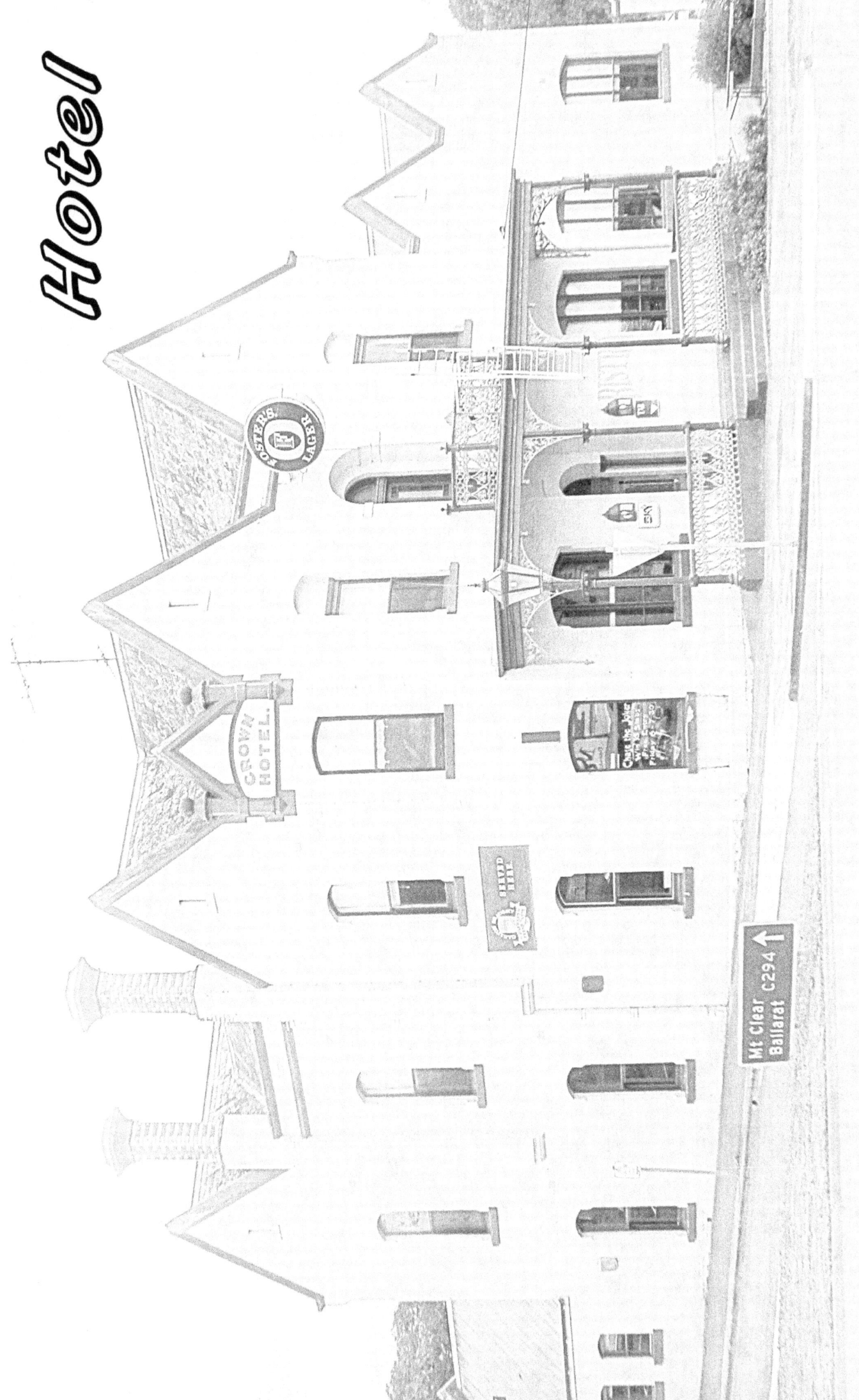

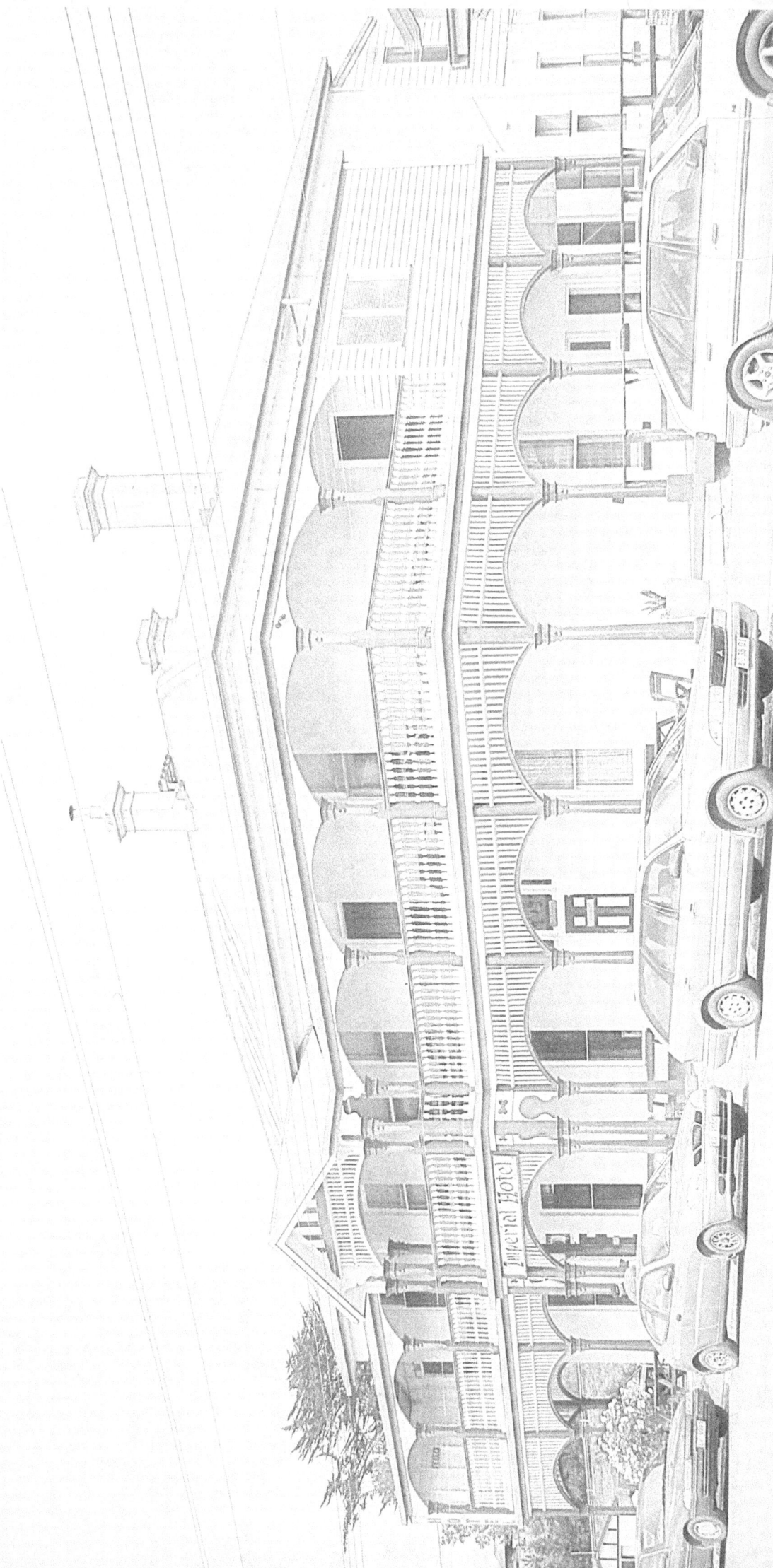

Hotel

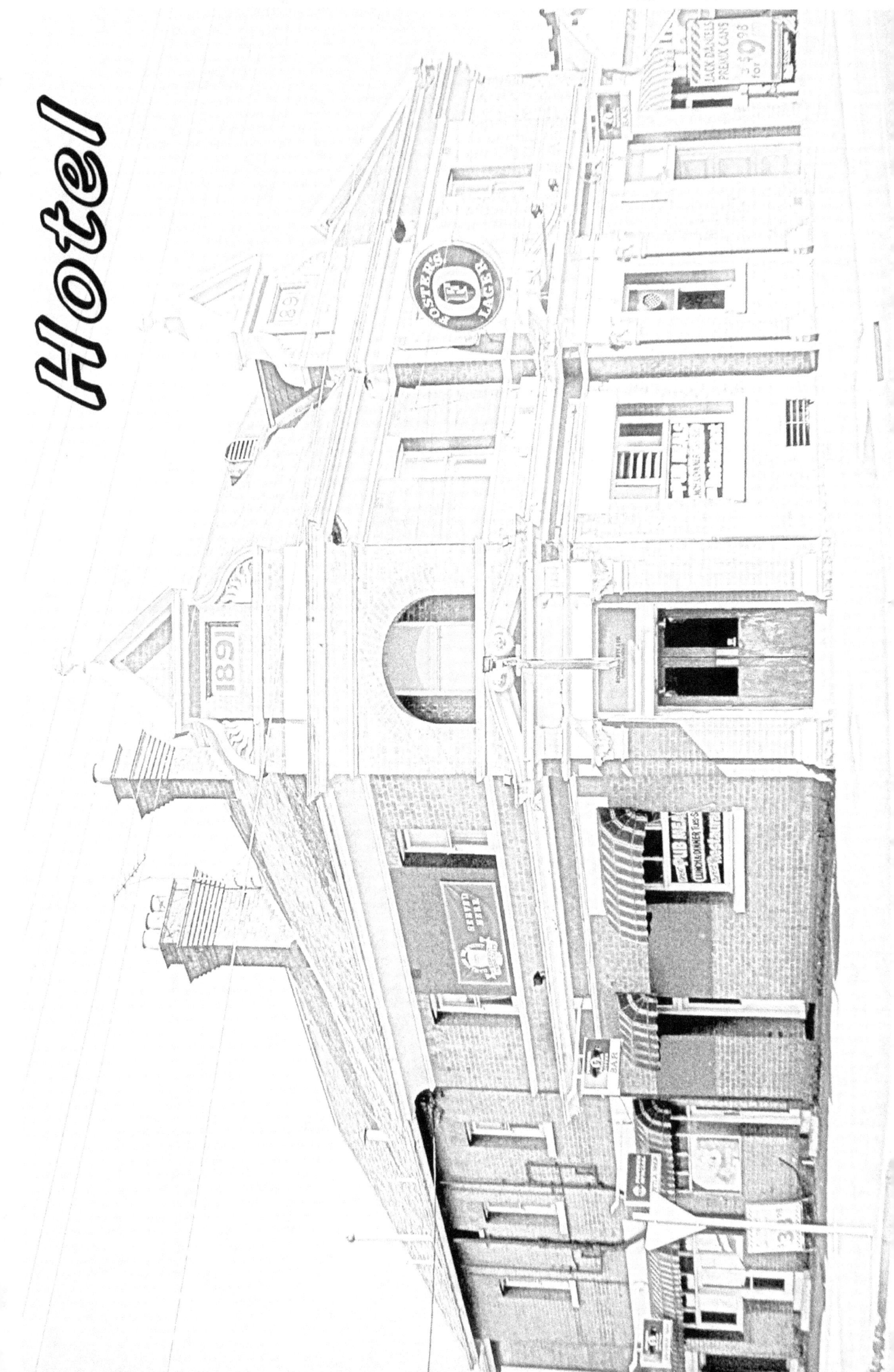

Hotel

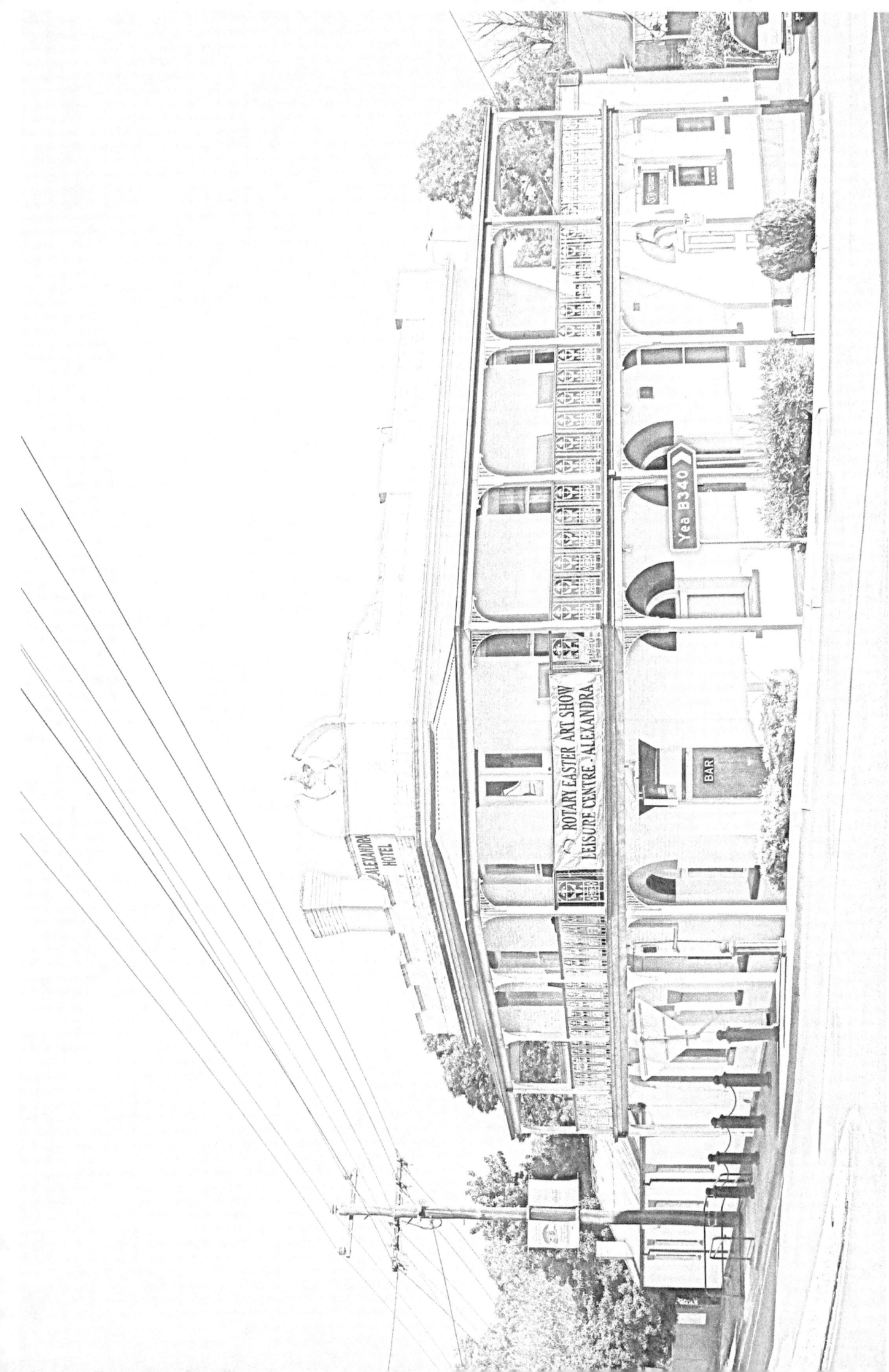

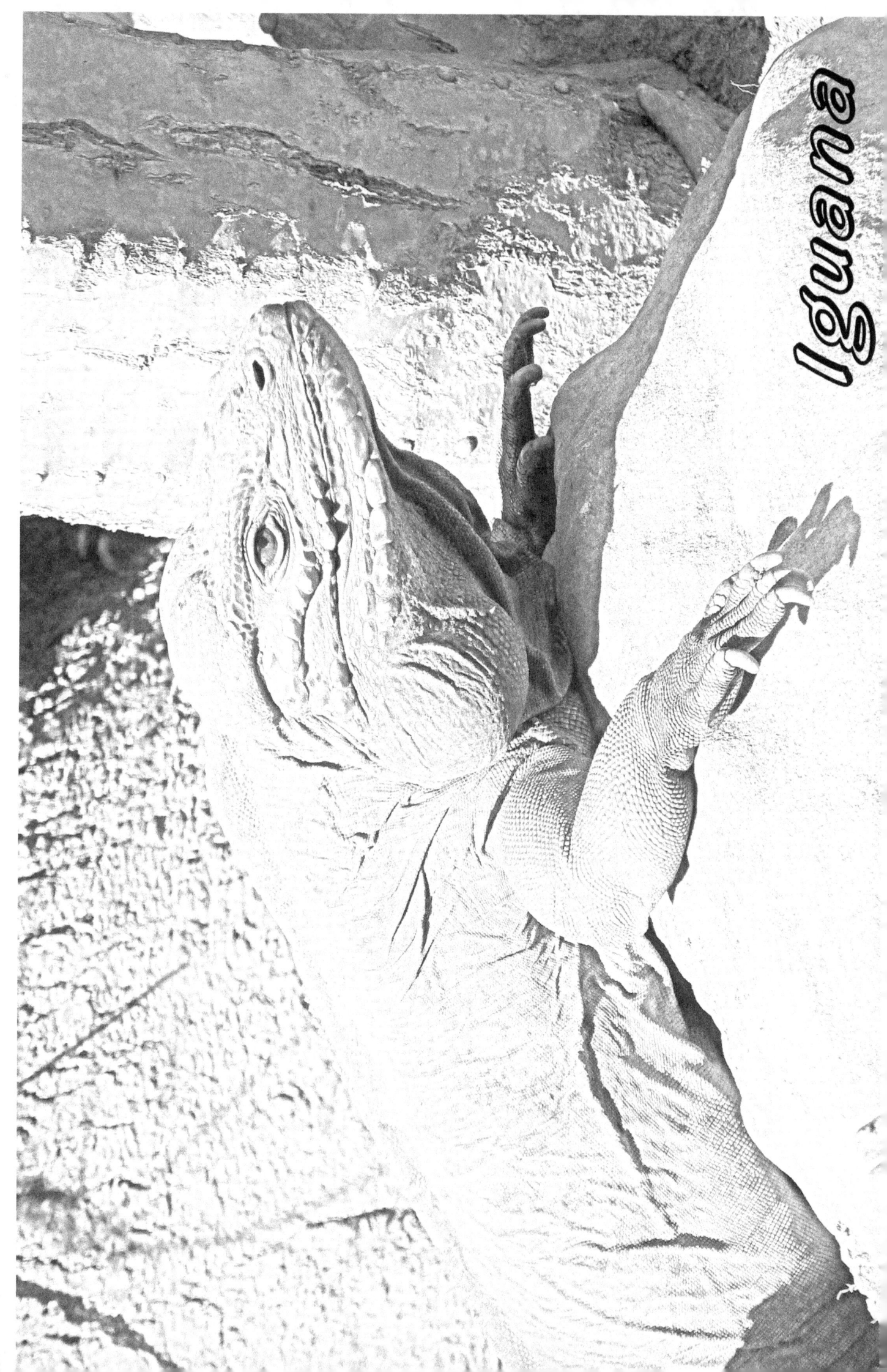

Iguana

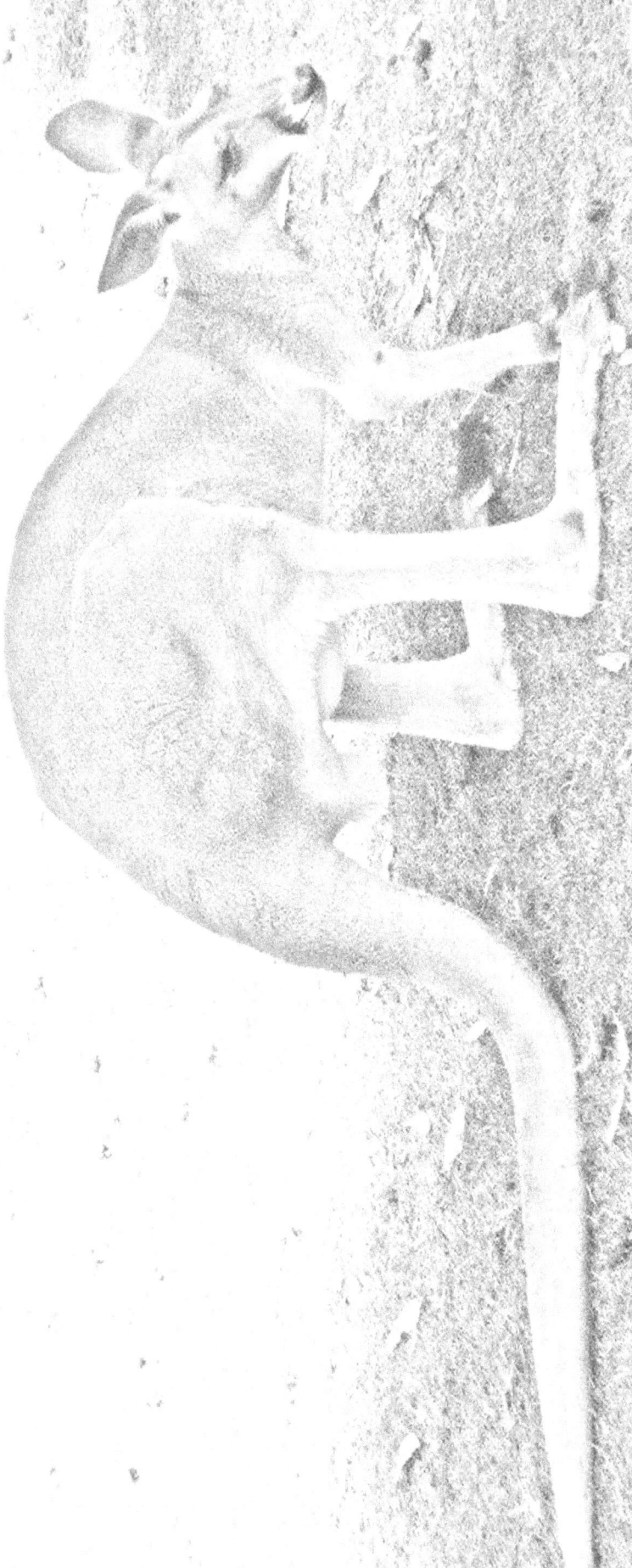

Kangaroo

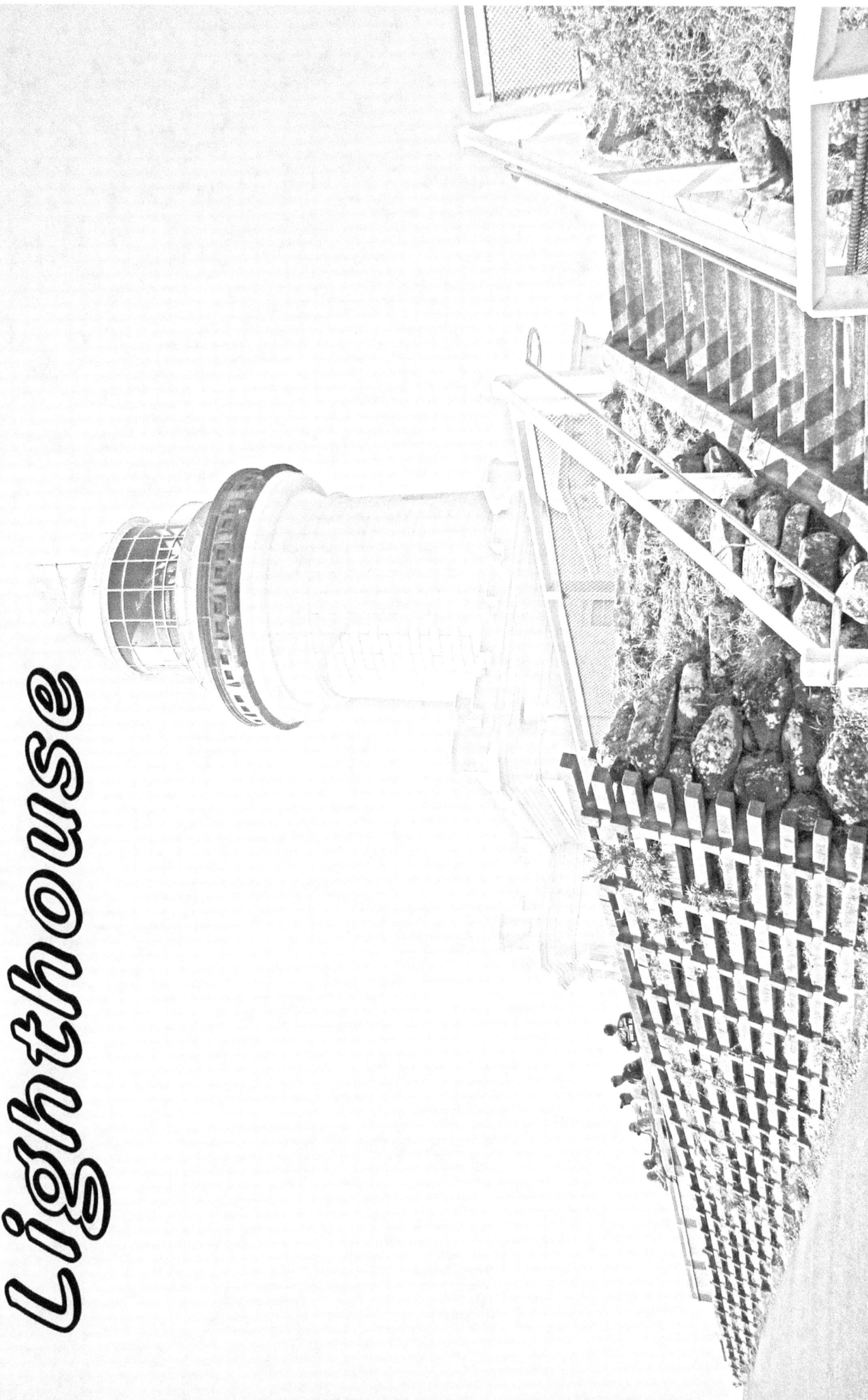

lighthouse

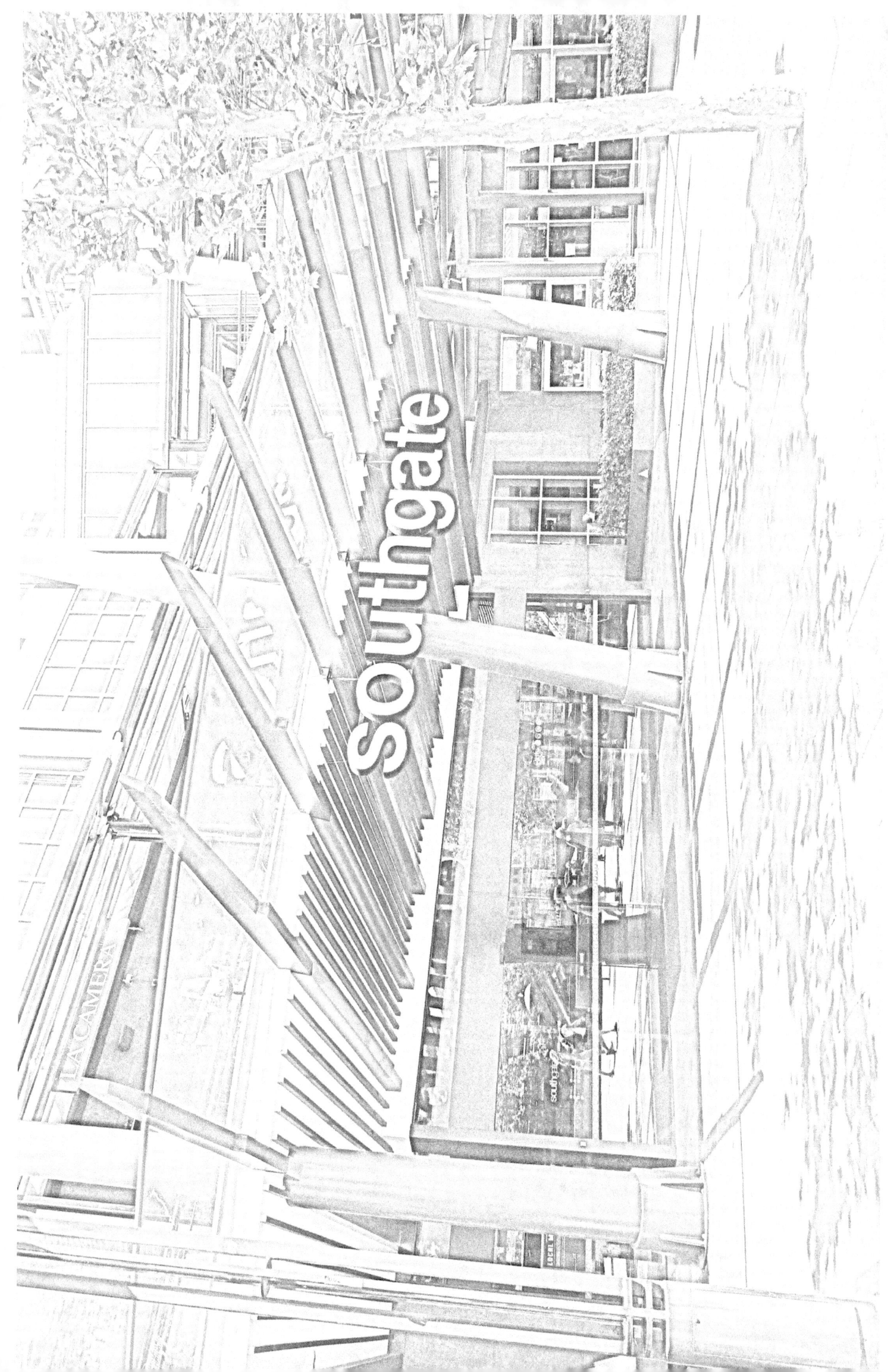

Parrots

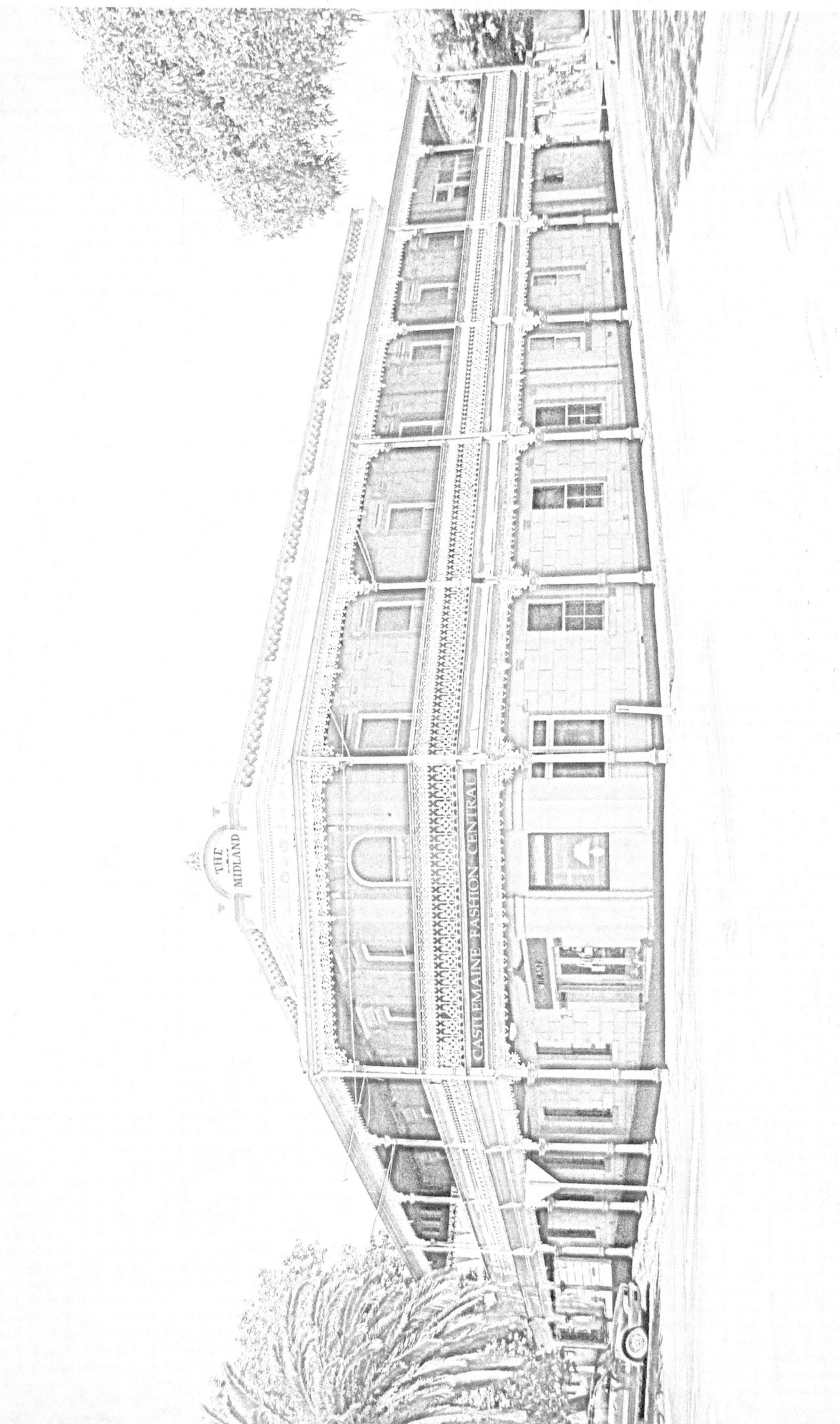

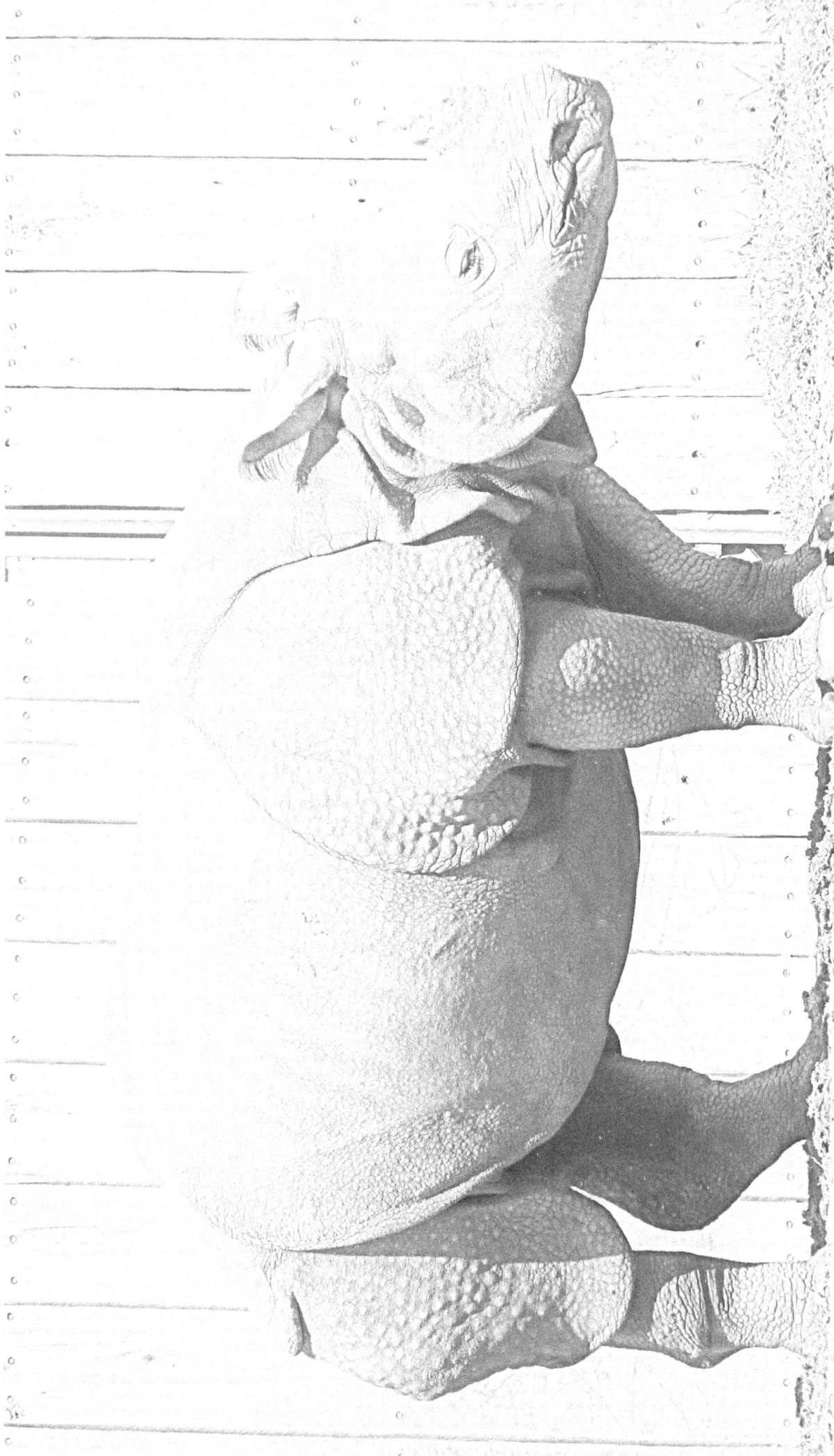

Rhino©

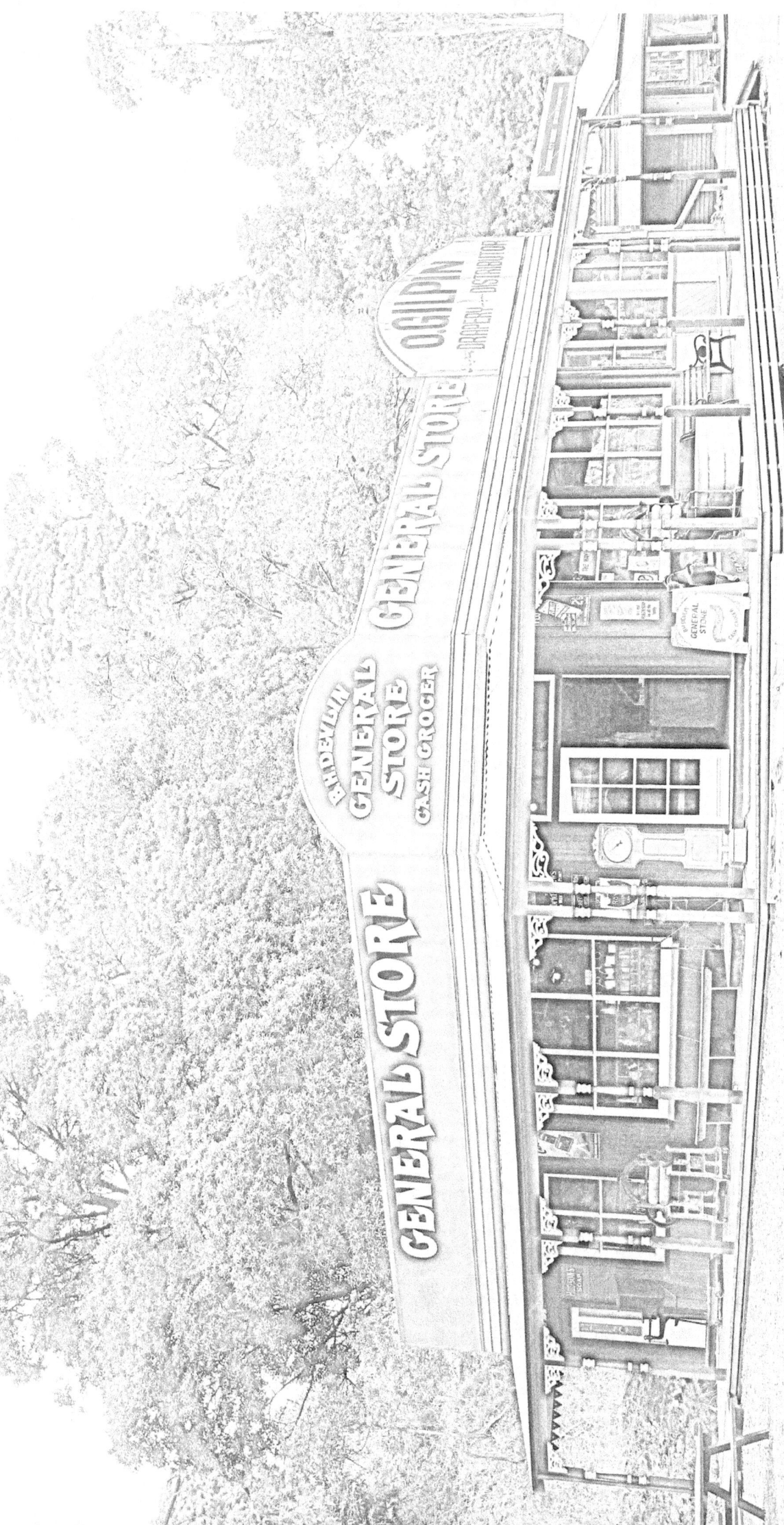

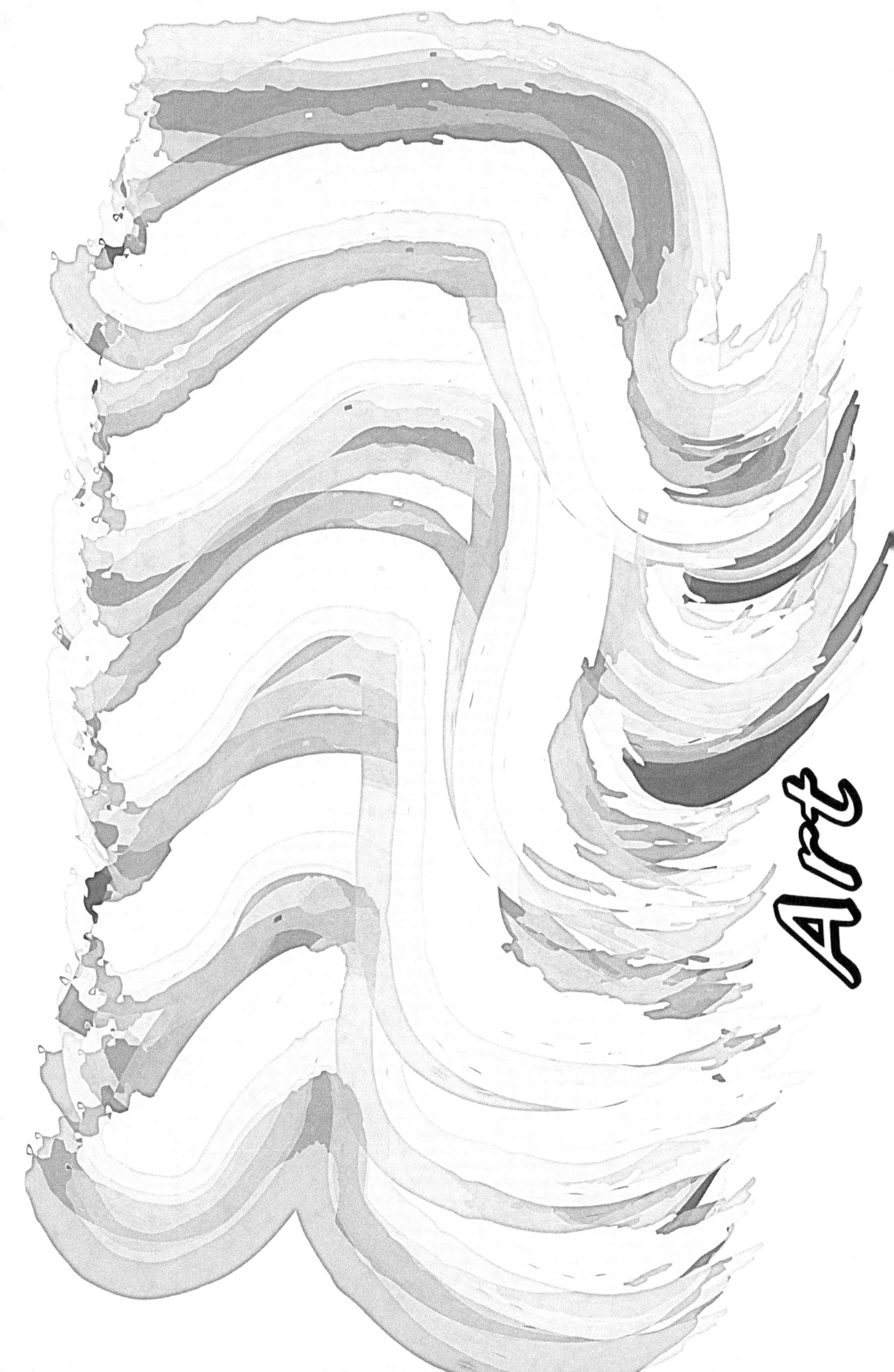

Snake

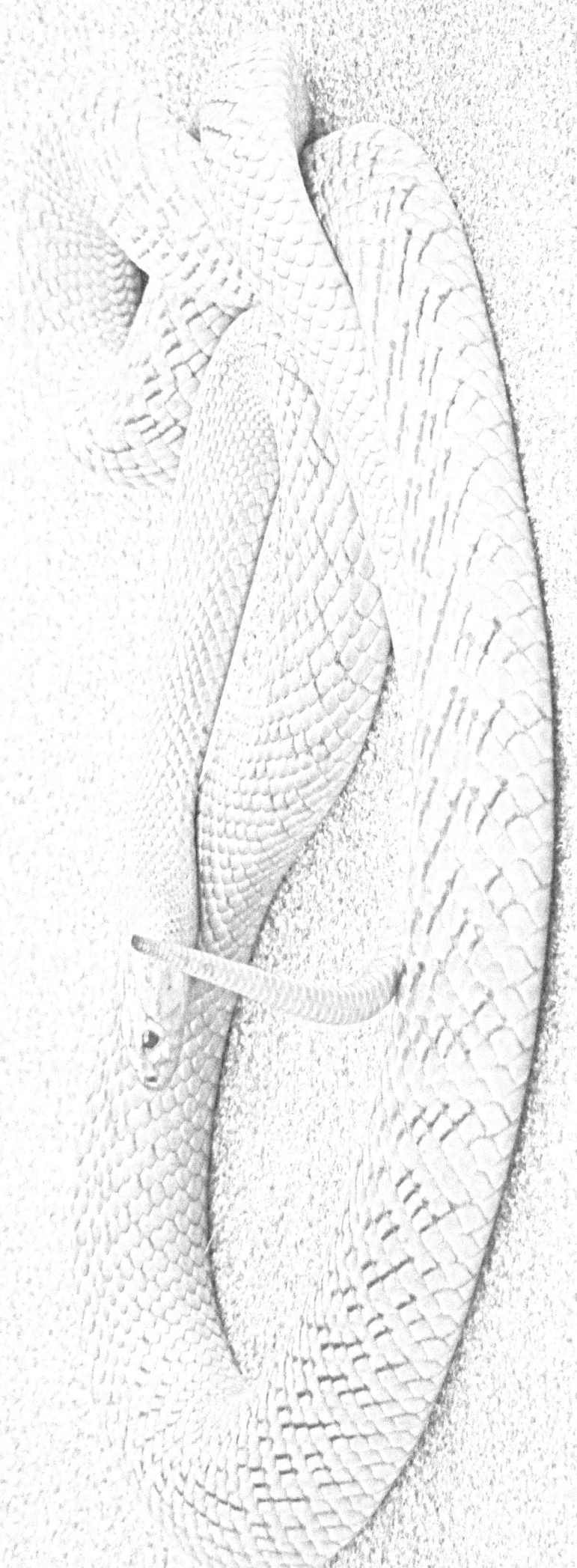

Steam Engine

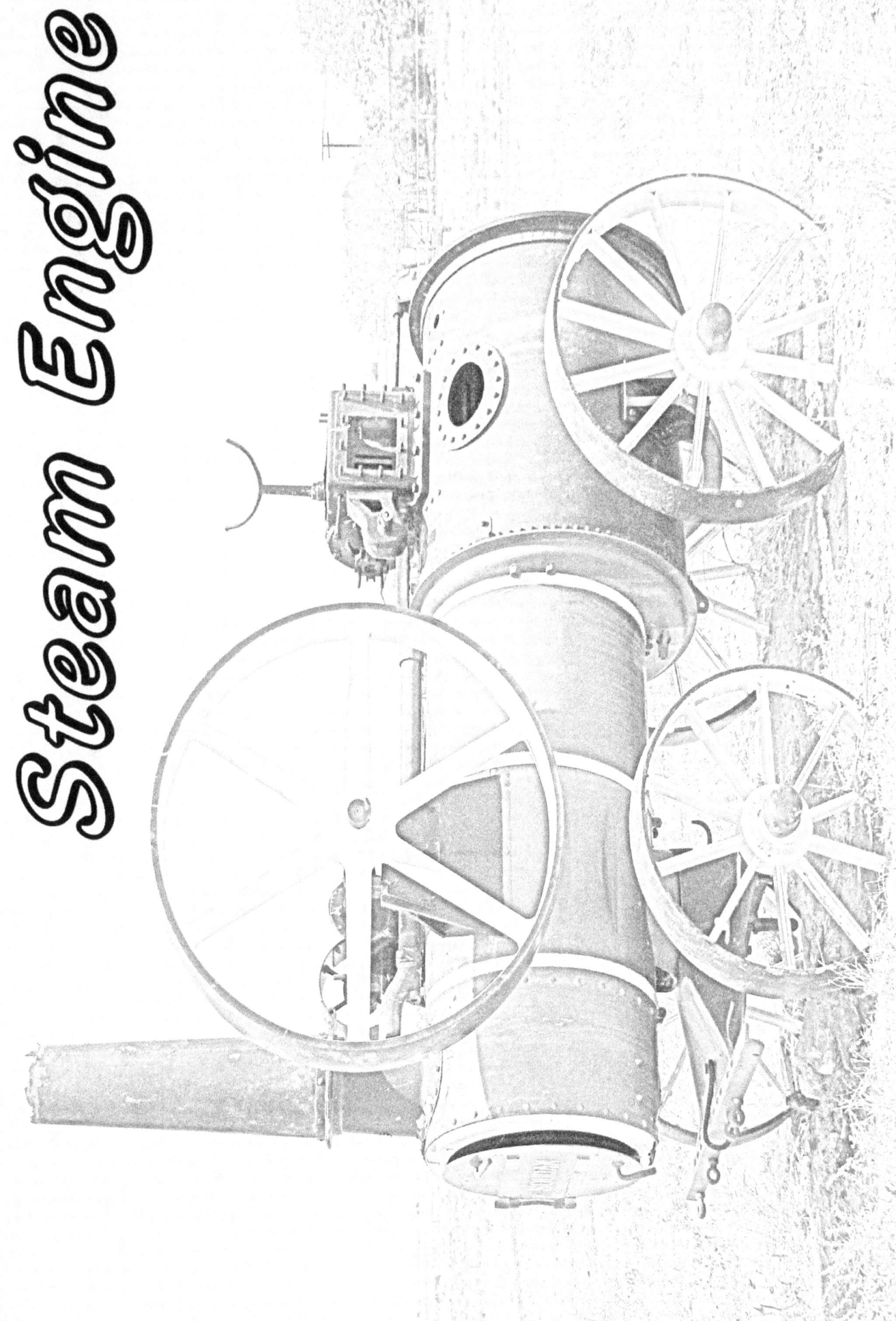

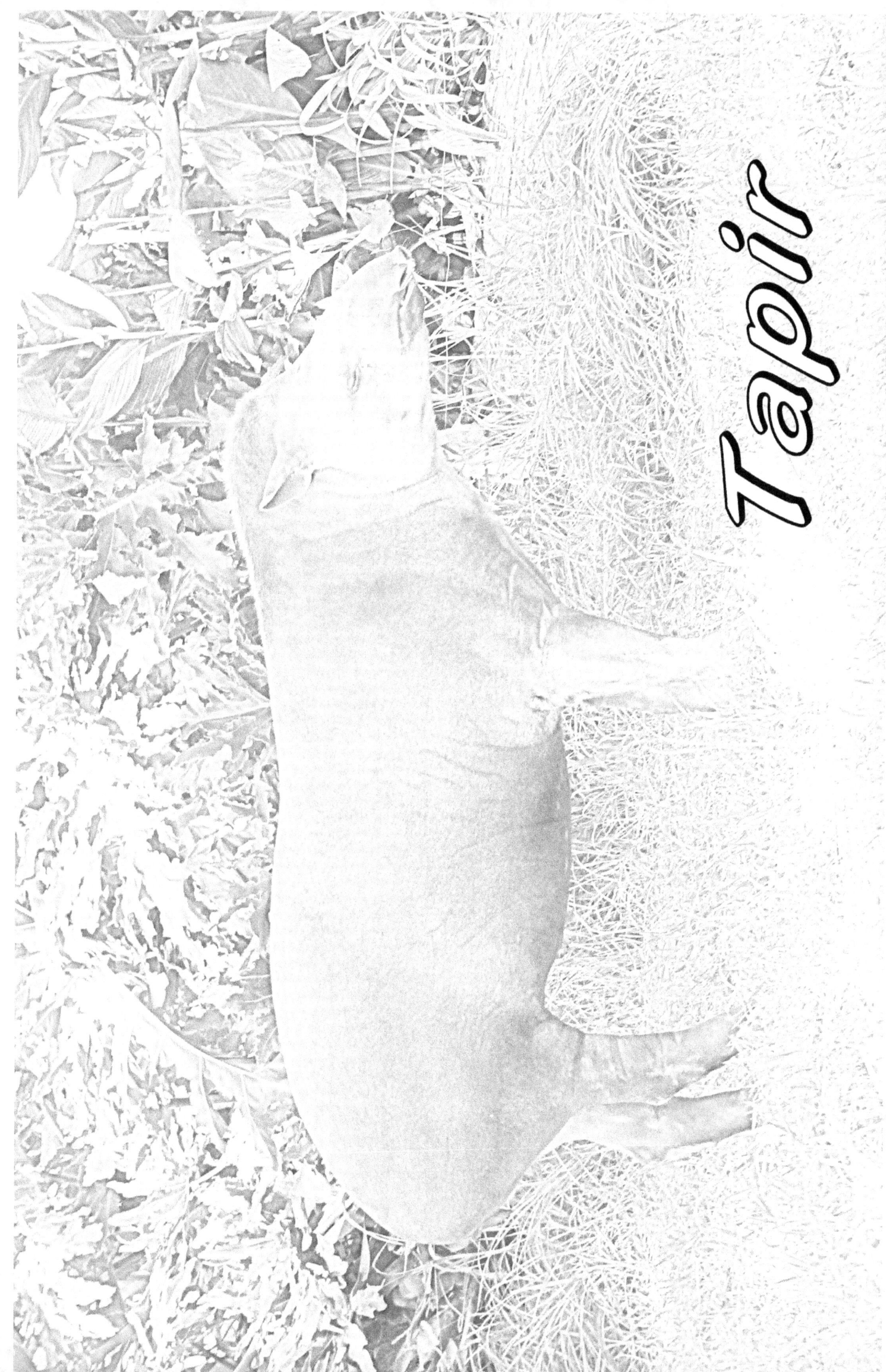

Tapir

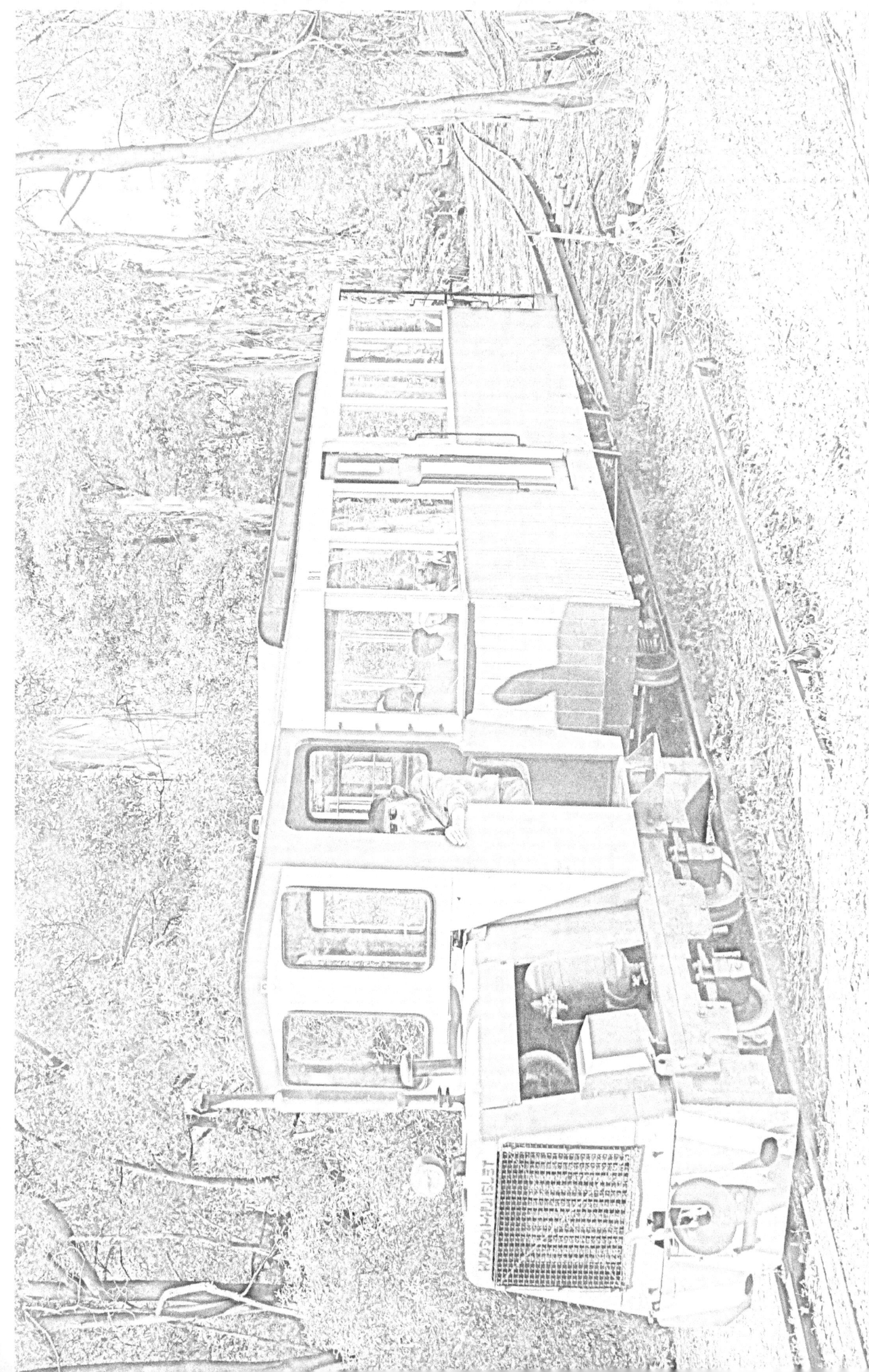

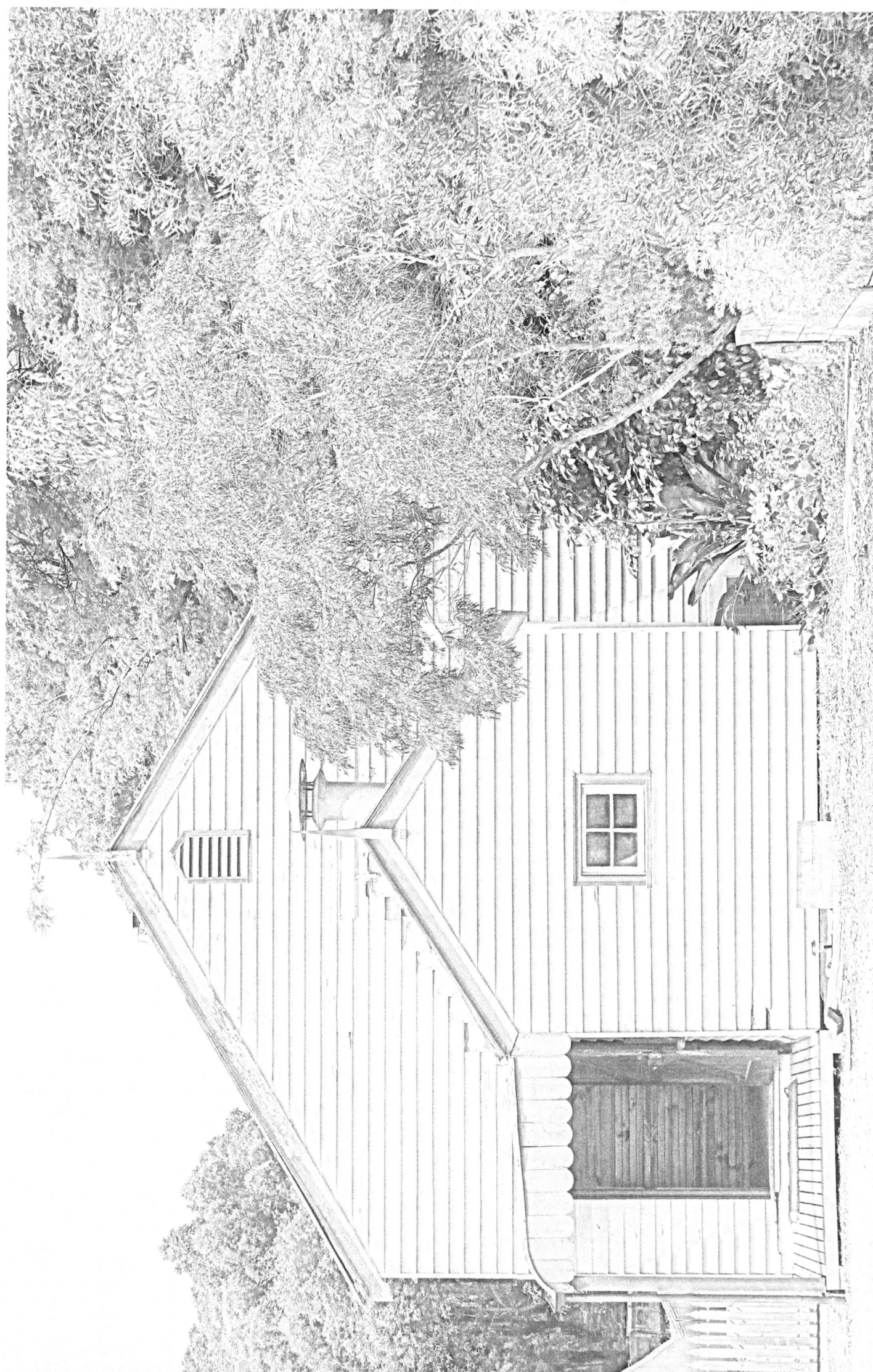

Steam Train

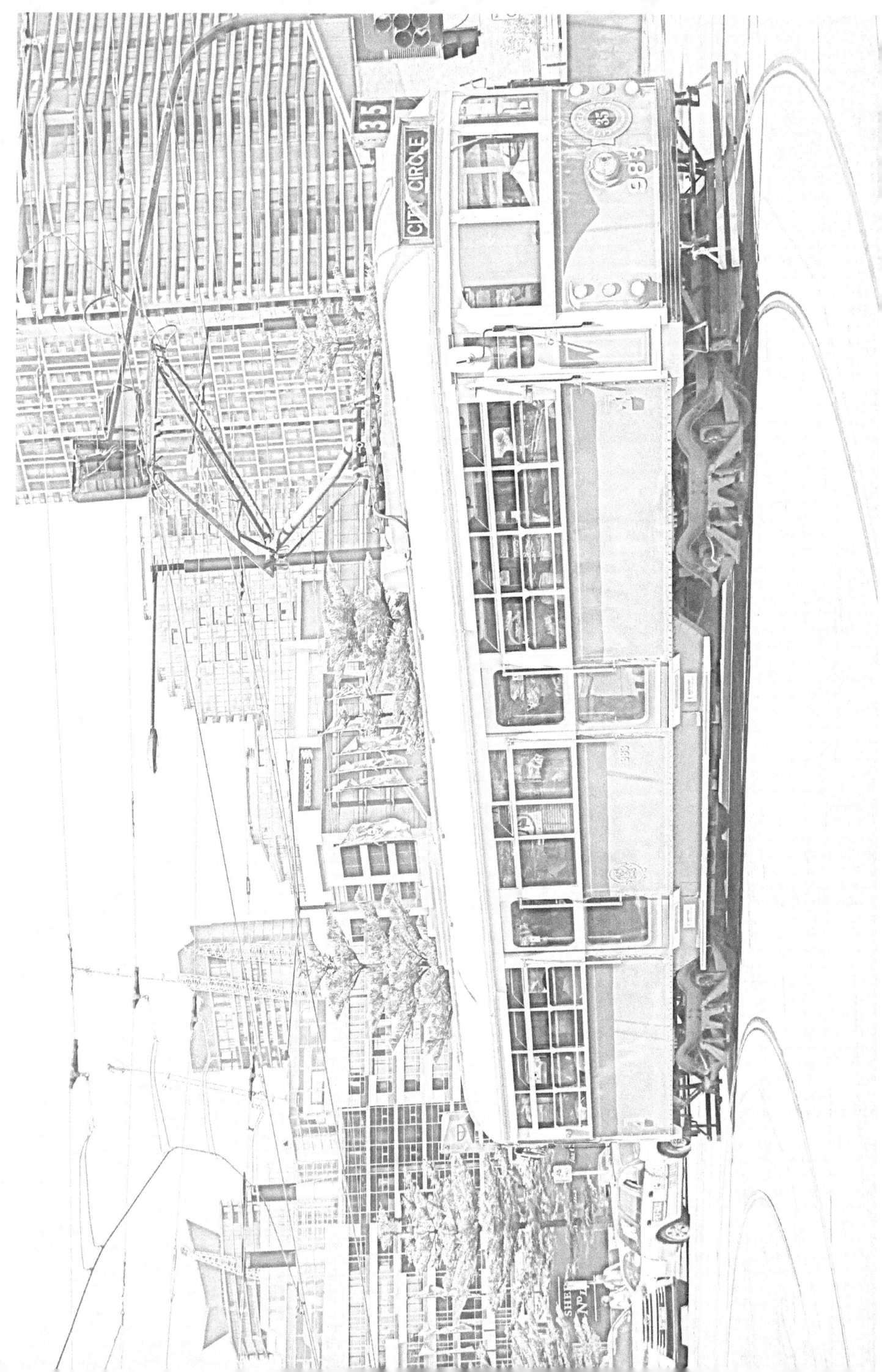

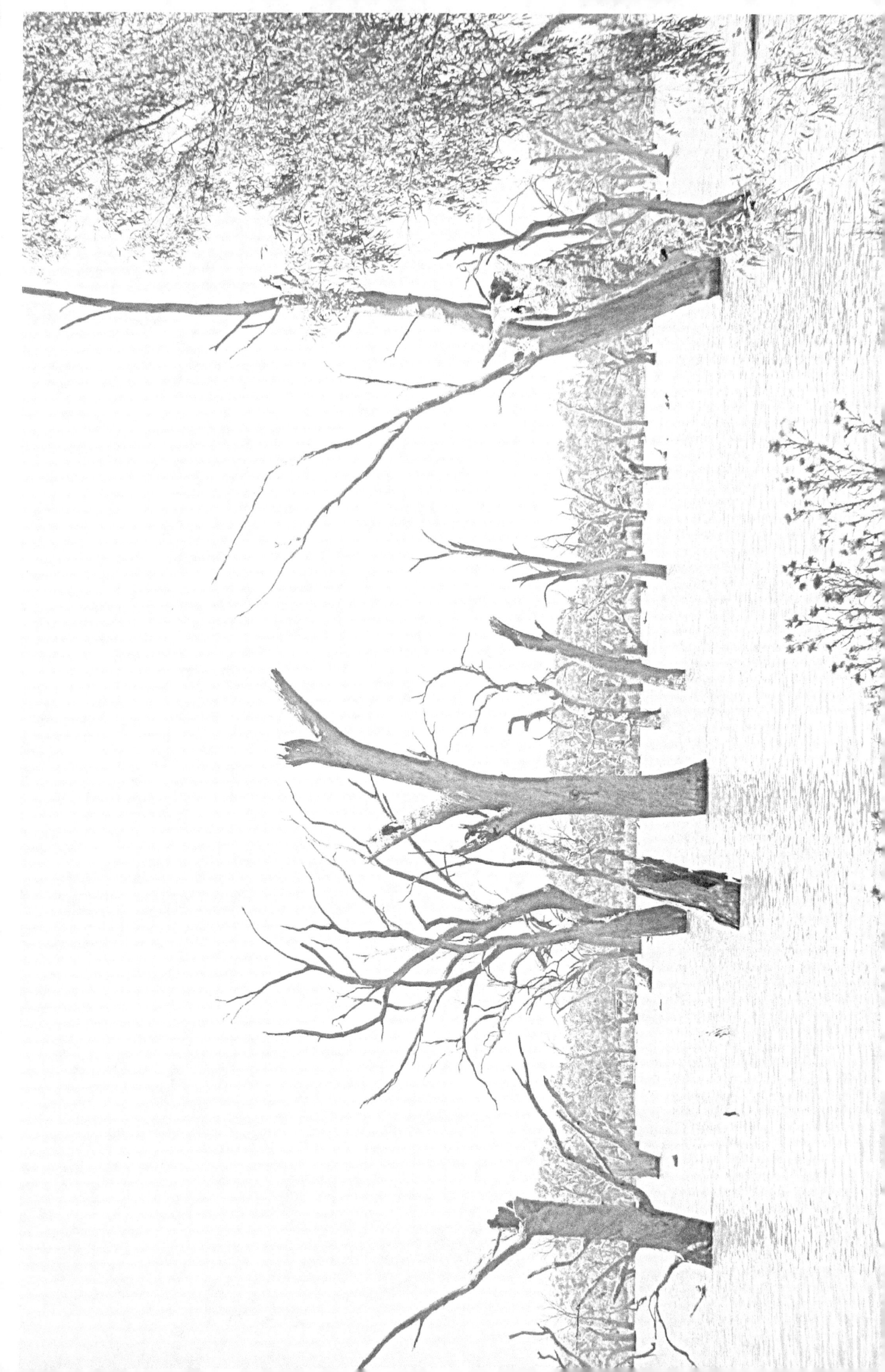

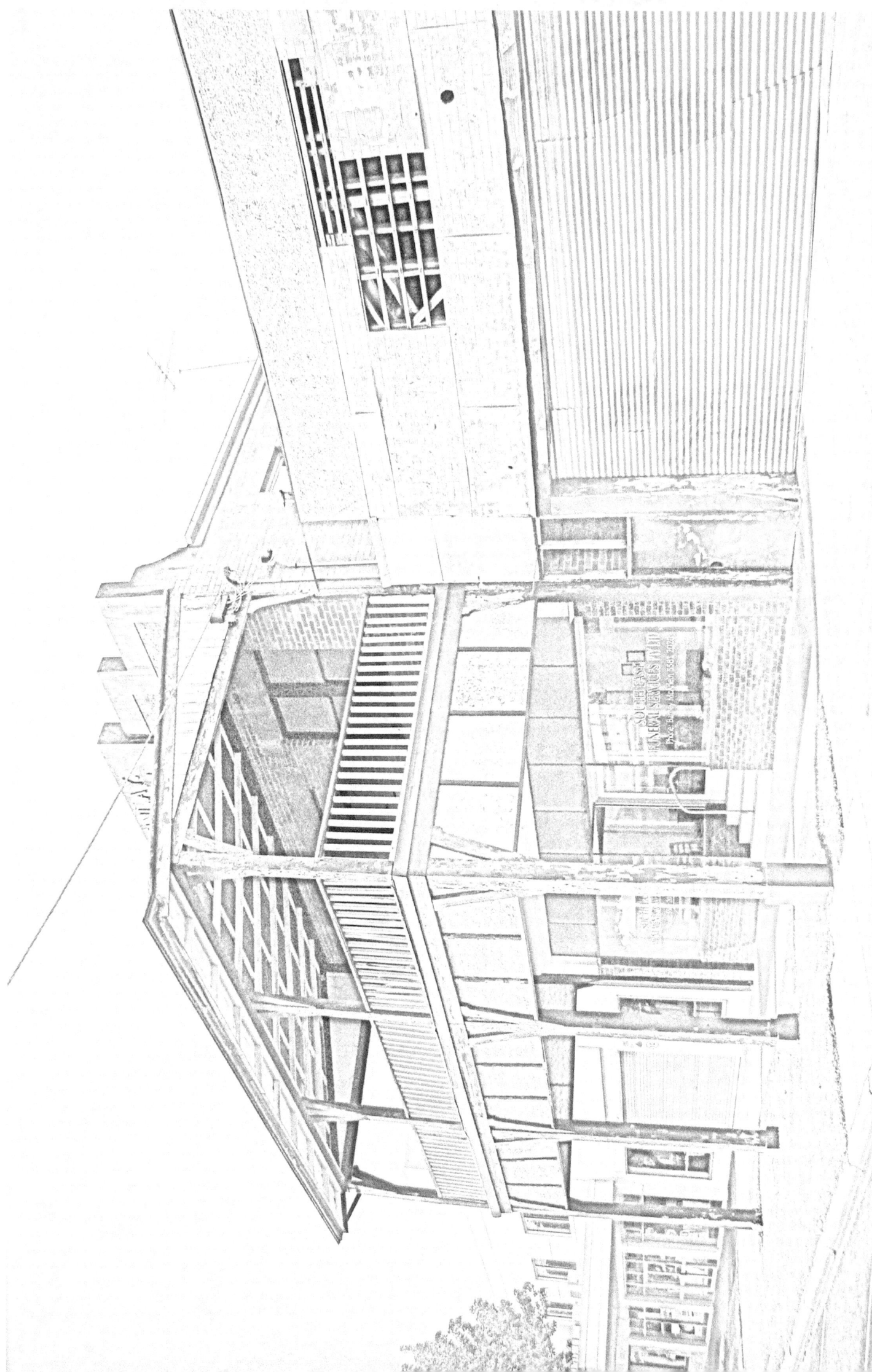

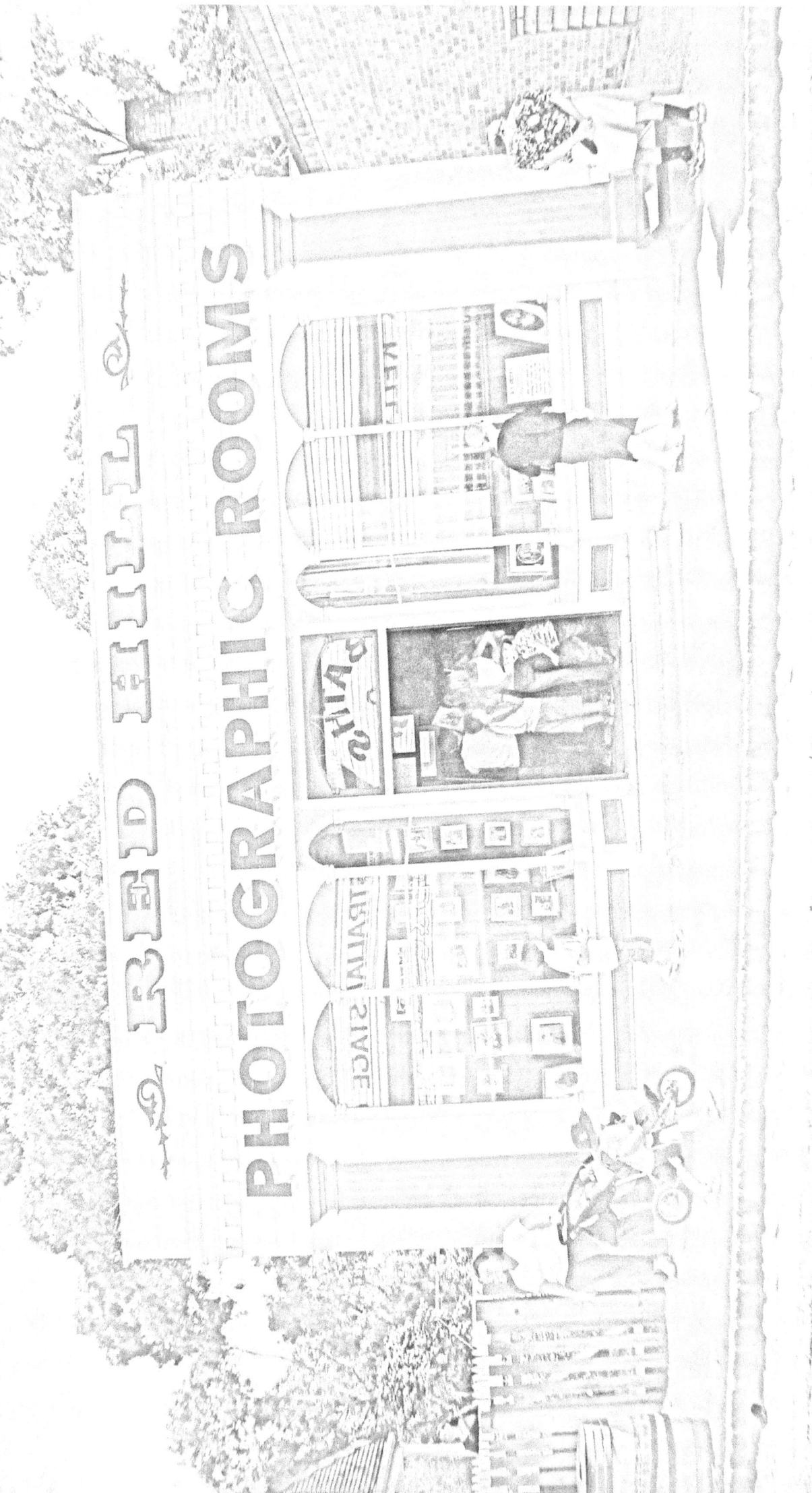

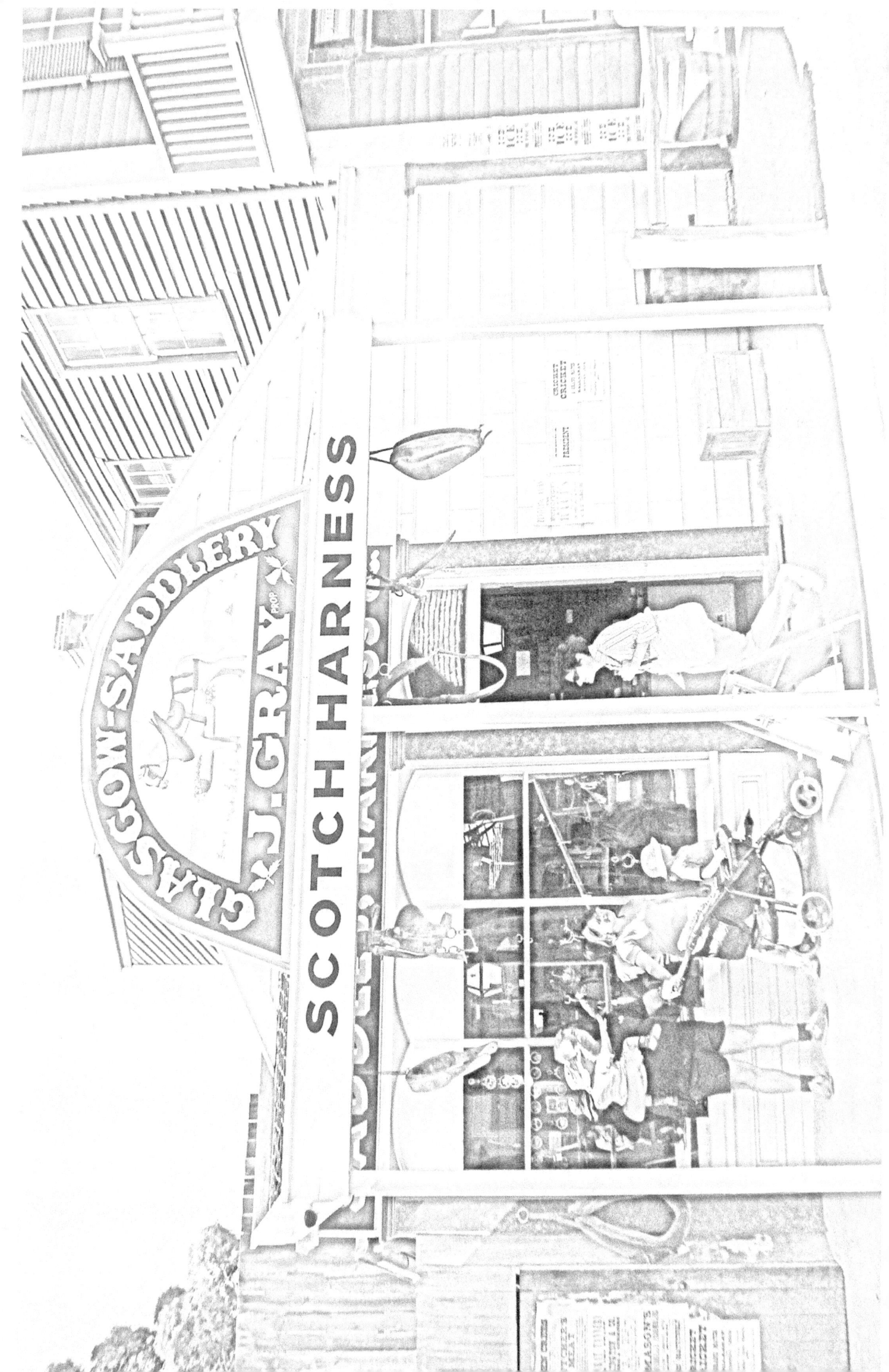

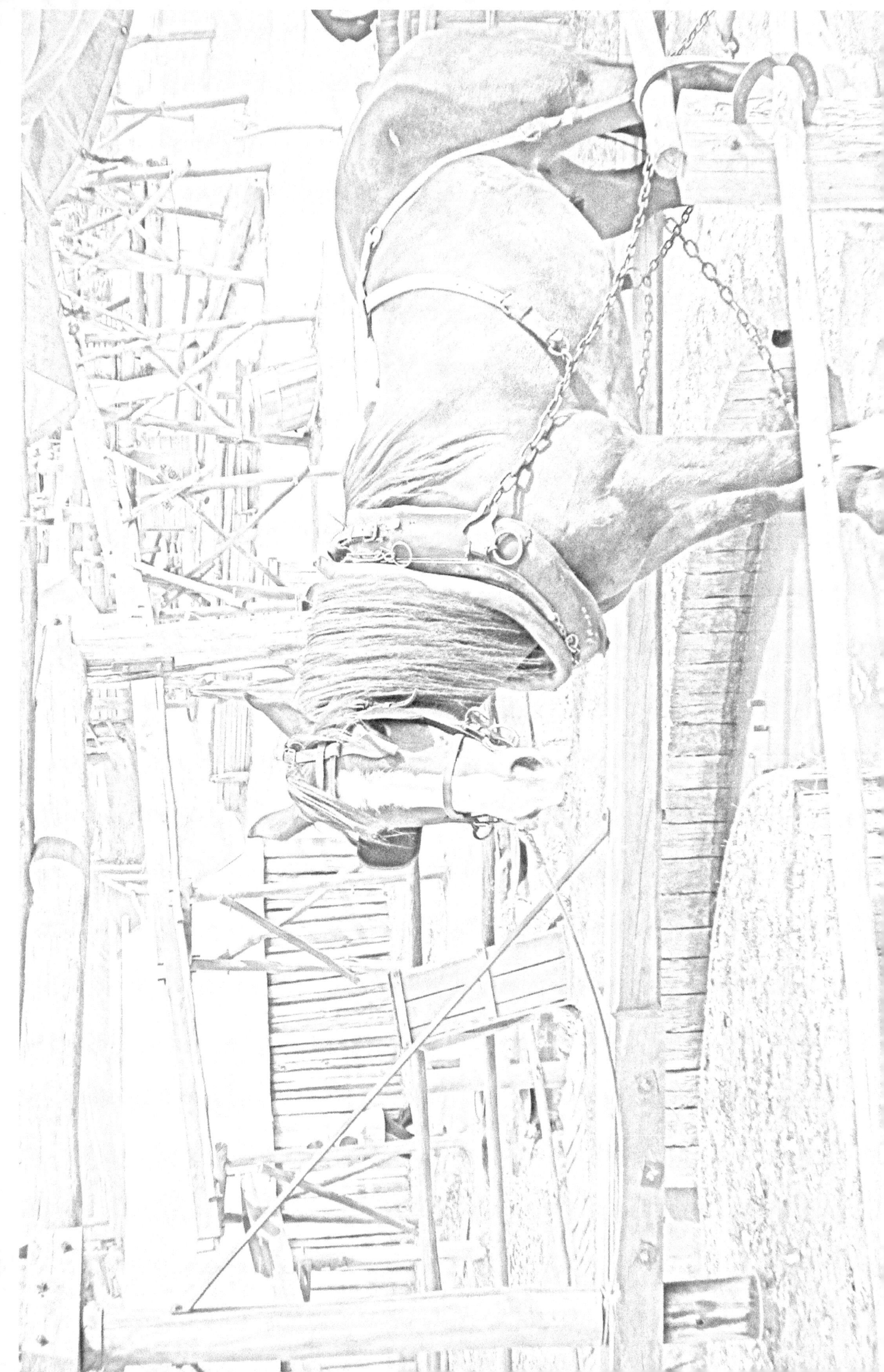

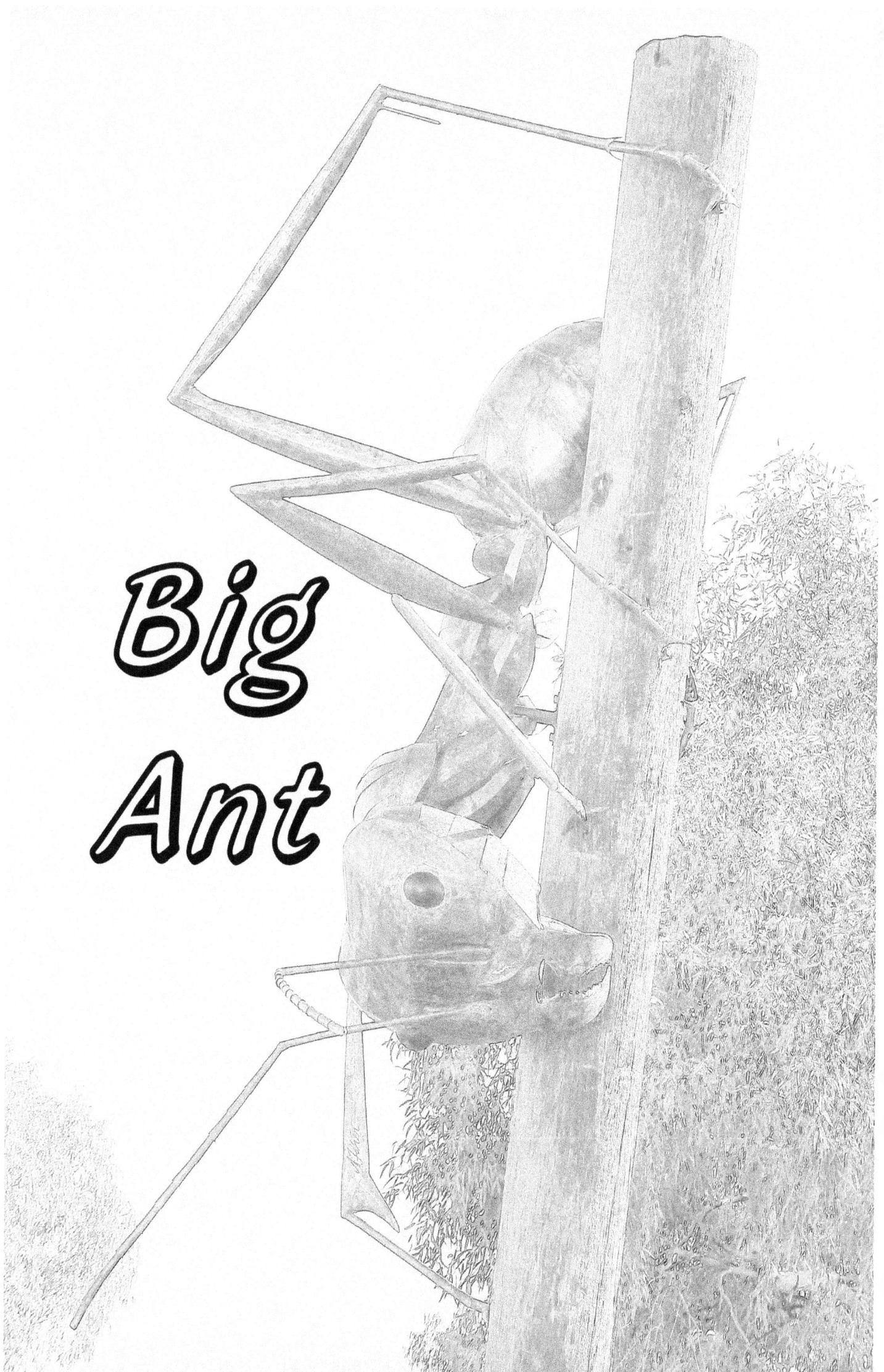

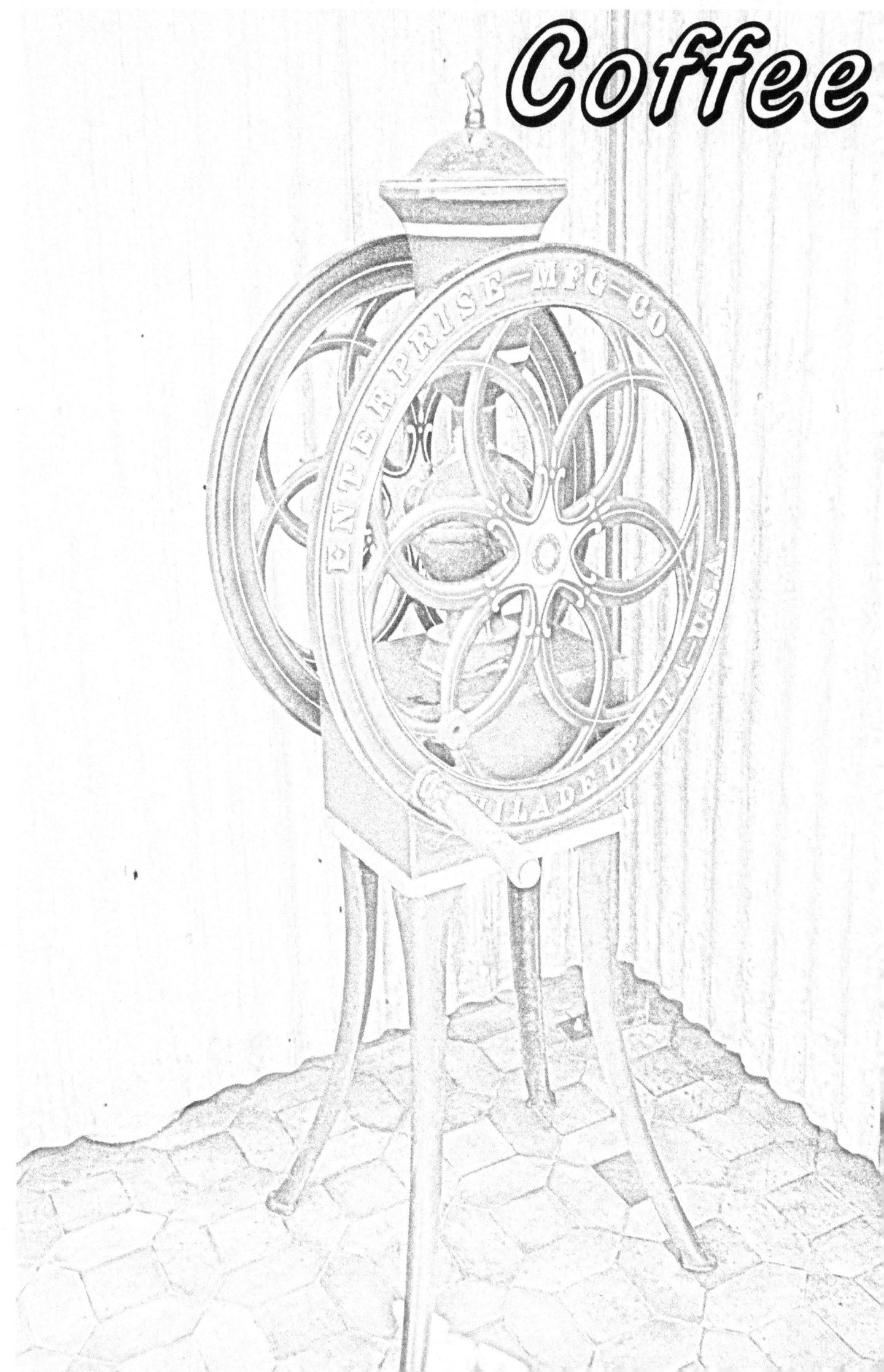

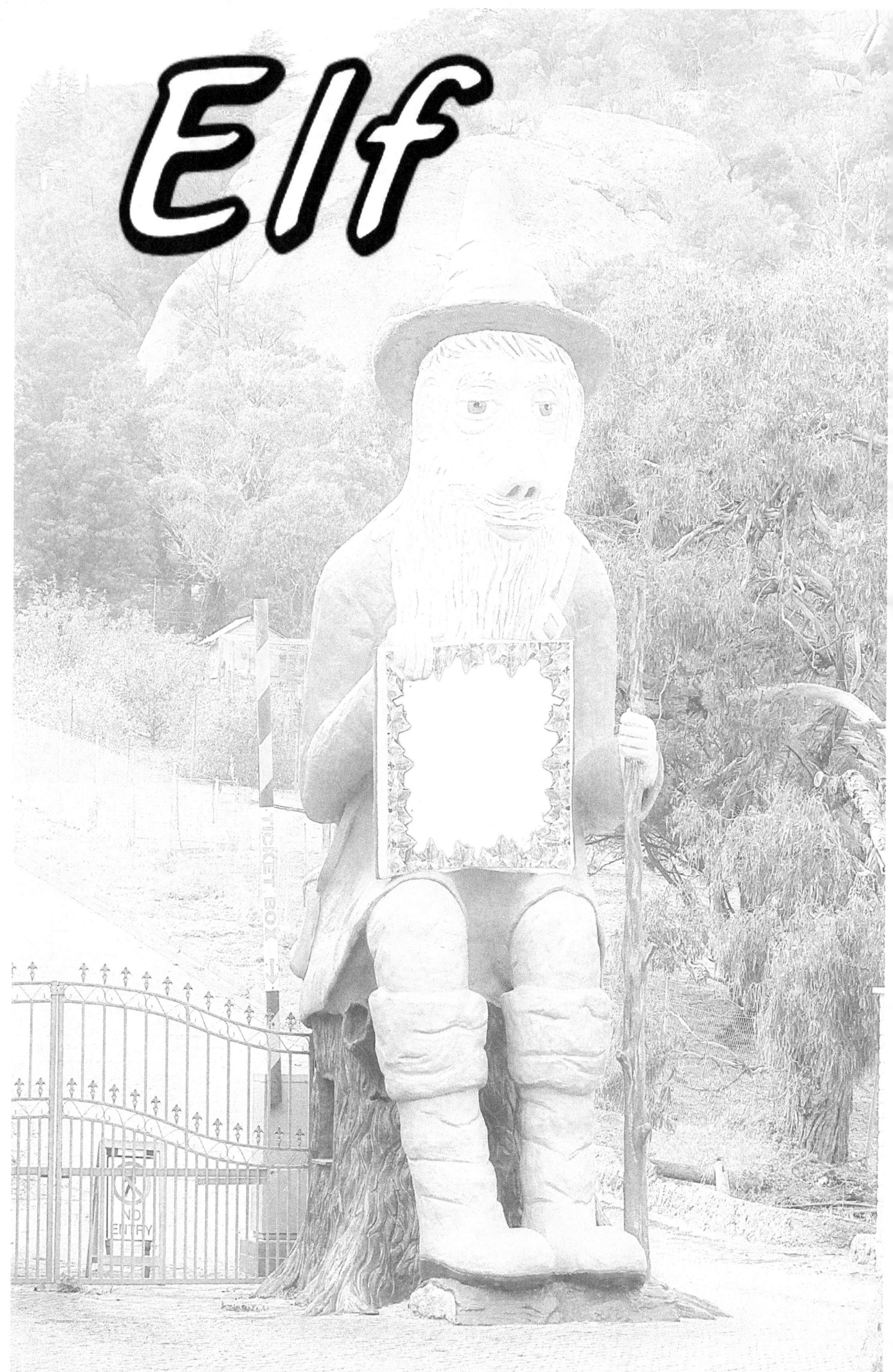

Elf

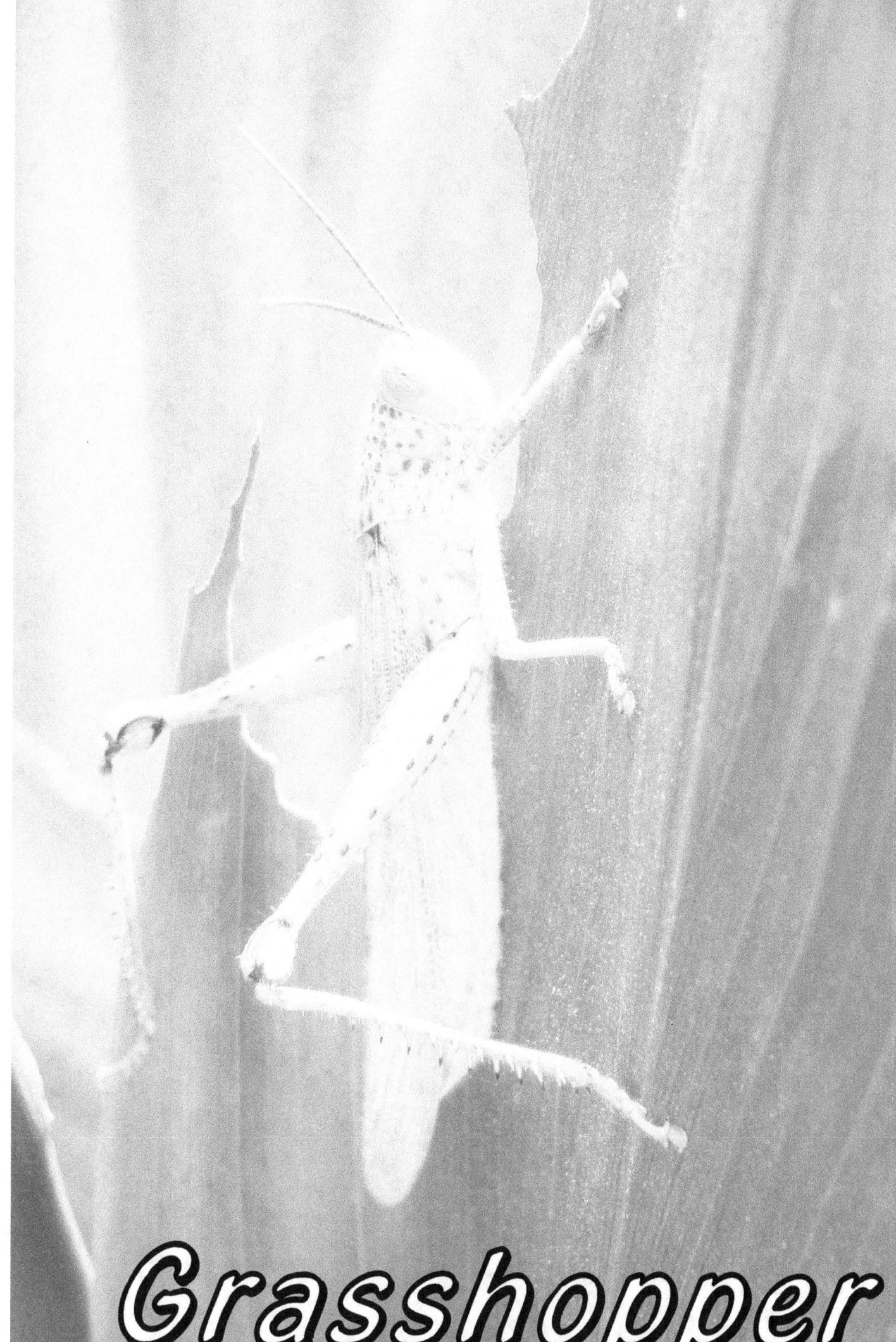

Grasshopper

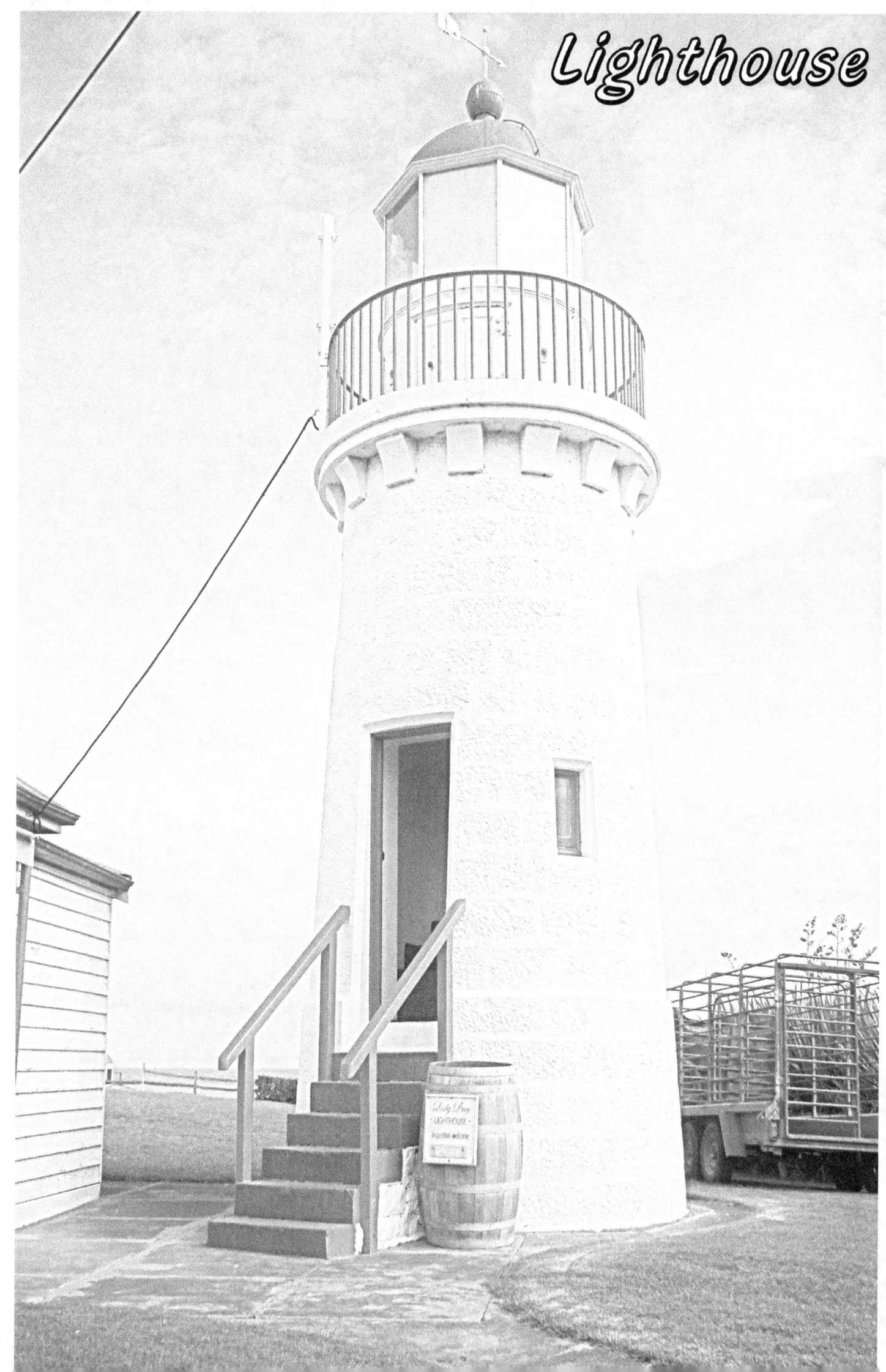

Lighthouse

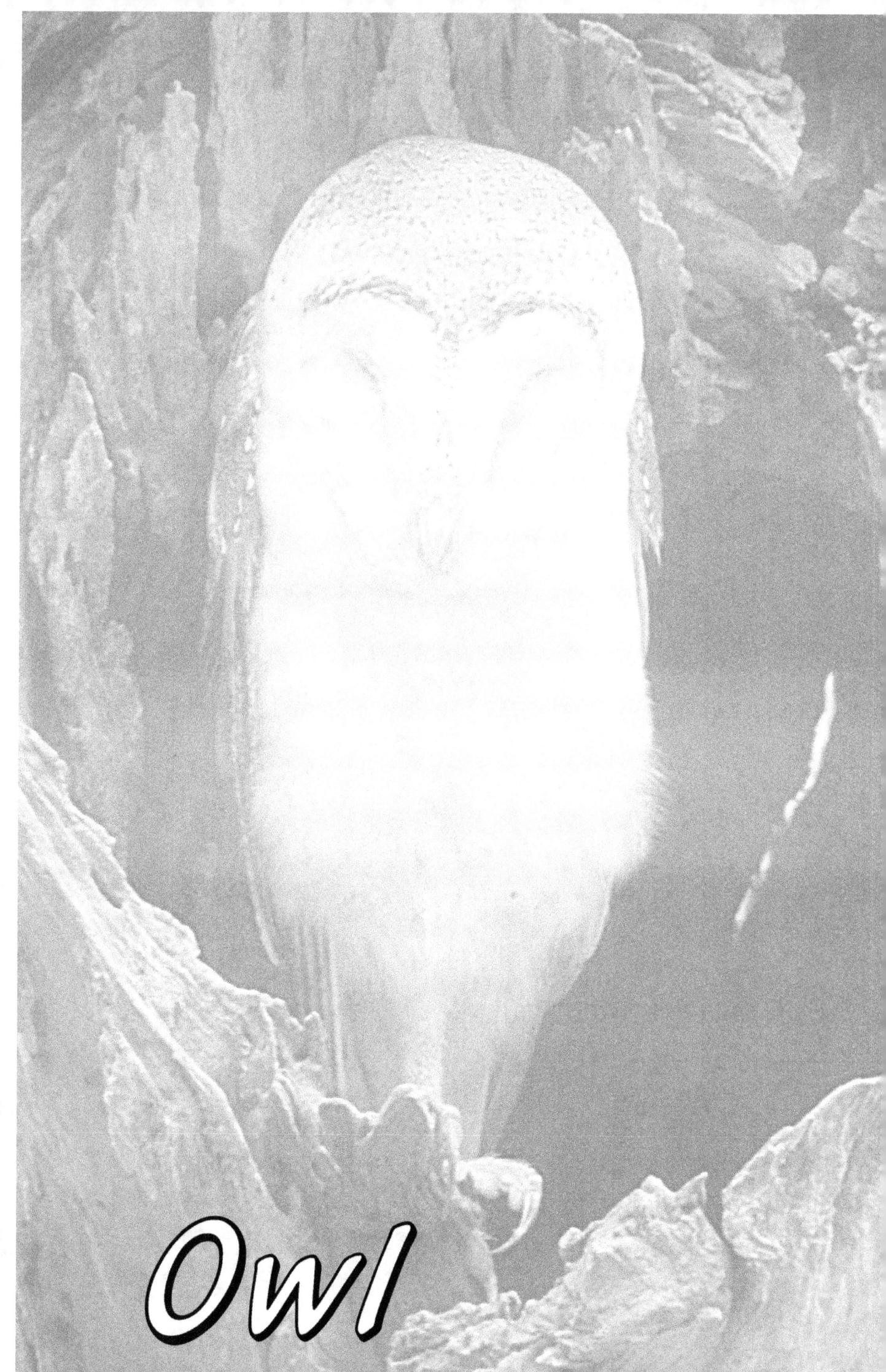

Owl

Seahorse

www.ingramcontent.com/pod-product-compliance
Lightning Source LLC
Chambersburg PA
CBHW081047180526
45170CB00005B/1727